# The "Do Do Not" Outlook

T0272788

## 77 Steps to Living an Extraordinary Life

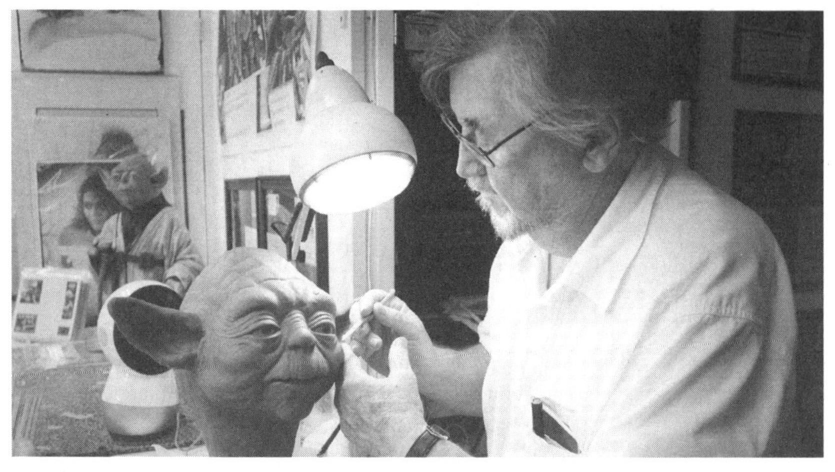

Nick Maley (That Yoda Guy)

**THE "DO OR DO NOT" OUTLOOK:**
**77 Steps to Living an Extraordinary Life**

All marketing and publishing rights guaranteed to and reserved by:

LIGHT
WORLD

721 W. Abram Street
Arlington, TX 76013
(800) 489-0727
(817) 277-0727
(817) 277-2270 (fax)
E-mail: info@fhautism.com
www.fhautism.com

© 2019 Nick Maley

Extended edition. All rights reserved.
Printed in the USA.

No part of this product may be reproduced in any manner whatsoever without written permission of Light World, Inc., except in the case of brief quotations embodied in reviews or unless noted within the book.

ISBN: 9781949177077

Dedicated to everyone with the inclination to read this book and the tenacity to pursue their dreams.

Looking for a Table of Contents? This isn't a normal book!
Flip to the back if you want a Book Guide—
otherwise, just read from the beginning to end.

# INTRODUCTION

I didn't set out to develop a philosophy or plan to create a foundation encouraging youngsters (and oldsters) to live extraordinary lives. Somehow, it just evolved.

**It all began when I was thirteen. A teacher told me I was an idiot and would work in a factory.** My struggle to overcome negativity and prove that teacher wrong began there. The concepts outlined in these pages are based on my journey through years of adversity, doubts, fears, mistakes, and triumphs. They were sharpened by the opportunities I grasped, the challenges I faced, and the life I lived. These principles took me from low-income housing to the making of ***Star Wars*** and sixty other movie and music projects. It was a journey through diverse endeavors and fanciful ambitions to my Caribbean adventures on Planet Paradise. I am fortunate to have lived life the way I wanted. Now I'm trying to share what I learned with another generation.

Someone reading this might mistakenly think I'm declaring war on society. I'm not. Without the millions of "normal" people who set the bar for accepted standards, there would be no level by which to measure my own accomplishments. I am ***not*** putting those people down in any way; but I ***am*** trying to put the typical views of the general public in perspective for others who, like me, prefer to live a less-conventional life.

I didn't want to bore the reader, so I limited most chapters to one page. Don't try to absorb the whole book in one reading. **It is important that you use this as part of a daily ritual. Read one page every day. When you reach the end, start again ... until you achieve your goal. Then make a new goal and start over!** Headings and passages in bold are intended to help you through your challenges. Use the blank pages to make your own related notes and lists (use pencil so you can make adjusts over time). Break your notes into small, detailed steps so that they are easier to achieve.

If you are ever tempted to give up, **be sure you read the "final thoughts"** before doing so.

Make of this book what you will. Take it or leave it. But ironically, although my journey started thirteen years before we made *Star Wars*, **the essence of these writings is undoubtedly within Yoda's most famous words ...**

**"Do or do not. There is no try."**

*"Where there's a Whill, there's a way."*

# CORE PRINCIPLES

Your Notes

# 1

## YOU CAN'T LIVE AN EXCEPTIONAL LIFE BY BEING "NORMAL"

If you take nothing else from this book, grasp this.

It's ***normal*** to follow standards and examples set by the people around you. It's normal to go to school and want to fit in with your friends. It's normal to have the same interests as your associates and to absorb the negativity of popular wisdom. It's normal to adopt the limited expectations that society considers safe options. **But let's not forget that another word for "normal" is average, or ordinary**—and average people get killed in video games! If you want to be that ordinary individual, that's okay. Hang out with your friends, do what they do, and you will be the same as everybody else.

The bottom line is, **you can't be normal and exceptional at the same time. You have to be one or the other.** And once you accept the regular path to mediocrity then, as Yoda would say, "forever will it dominate your destiny."

But if you think BIG, then go change the world and let your friends follow ***you***.

Your Notes

*"People who want to stretch beyond the norm shouldn't take advice from people who can't imagine that such a thing is possible."*

*— Nick Maley*

# 2

## IF YOU DON'T INVEST IN YOUR IMPOSSIBLE DREAMS, YOU ARE THE ONE WHO GUARANTEES THEY WON'T COME TRUE

The world is filled with negative opinions from people who assume you will make no more effort than the people around you. They are eager to tell you why you shouldn't bother to try to do something exceptional. But only you can determine what you will become, and if you don't invest the time to acquire the skills and contacts that can change your life, ***you* condemn yourself** to mediocrity.

I know those are hard words. But you need a hard push to overcome the huge influences that imply that it's smarter to take the path of least resistance, settle for less, and blend in with the crowd. **The truth is that *you can achieve anything* provided you stick at it long enough to make it happen.**

Oh, and you know that trendy guy or girl in class that others tend to listen to? Well, he or she has no more experience of life than you do.

## Your Notes

# 3

## THINK OF YOURSELF AS A TOOLBOX

Everything you learn to do is a tool within the toolbox you draw upon to get you through life. You start by learning to talk and walk. Those tools help you discover the world and interpret your experiences. The language tool helps you learn to read, and the reading tool opens a myriad of other topics. Sometimes you learn something with no concept of how you will use that tool. You will never know how combining two tools will solve a future problem, unless those tools are in the toolbox. **The more tools you have, the more resources you have to solve life's difficulties, the more useful you are to the people that you need to impress, and the more capable you are of reaching your ultimate goal.**

The world is ever-changing. Don't get left behind by not investing in newer tools. Whether you are sixteen or ninety-six, keep acquiring those tools. It will keep you current and it will keep you young.

Your Notes

# 4

# BUILD ON WHAT YOU HAVE THAT OTHERS DON'T

If you want to get opportunities that others don't, you need to be noticed. To do that, **you have to separate yourself from the crowd**. The easiest and quickest way to achieve that is to see which skills and assets you have that others around you don't and build on those.

It might be something you learned from family. It might be a talent you have or even a key interest that you are driven to develop further. Use all possible resources to hone your skills. If you don't have skills that are different from the people around you, look at what interests you and develop some.

**Build on what makes you different from your competition.**

**You need to be the red tree in the forest.**

Your Notes

# 5

## FOLLOW YOUR PASSION

I was at a convention in Germany, talking to my old friend Robert Watts, associate producer of the classic ***Star Wars*** trilogy and the first three ***Indiana Jones*** movies. Robert reinforced my belief that **if you have a passion for what you are doing, you are going to succeed because you put in more effort than someone who doesn't.**

Passion helps you persevere when obstacles get in your way. Passion helps you maintain the long haul that leads to success. If you don't have passion for what you do, if it's just a means to pay your bills, someone else with more passion will run right over you and leave you as an also-ran. As Robert says, "If you have the passion, you will succeed." Follow your passion through life. The reward of satisfaction is in itself a measure of success.

Your Notes

*“Wisdom is subjective. It's a matter of perspective. What is considered wise by some is a pessimistic limitation to another. A risk for one is a golden opportunity to the next. It’s all dependent upon your outlook on life.”*

*— Nick Maley*

# 6

## IF YOU ACCEPT OTHER PEOPLE'S NEGATIVITY, YOU ALLOW **YOUR** LIFE TO BE LIMITED BY **THEIR** LACK OF IMAGINATION

All too often, when you tell someone that you are hoping to do something beyond the norm, you are met with a barrage of negative opinions and advice to "play it safe." That's because they assume that if you strive for something exceptional, you will most probably fail. They will tell you why your dreams are not practical. They presume that you are not capable of making more effort than friends and neighbors or rising above normal standards.

**Just because they were too scared to follow their dreams, just because they chose not to make the effort to live an exceptional life, doesn't mean that you should do the same thing.**

Their advice is based on a fear that you will fall below average (normal). But that attitude limits you from living an exceptional life. Take a good look at the person who is giving you advice and ask yourself if you want to live ***their*** life. If you don't, why accept advice from them?

## Your Notes

# 7

## DEFINE YOUR GOAL ... MAKE A PLAN

It's important that you establish a goal, even if at first you just identify the industry that most interests you. You don't have to pinpoint a specific job initially. Being realistic, you don't know with any certainty where your chosen path will lead you or what unexpected opportunities will fire your passion along the way. But don't let that uncertainty stop you from embarking on your journey, because **without a goal you aren't going anywhere, you are just wasting time drifting from today's inconsequential events to tomorrow's inconsequential events.**

Define the destination you are striving for, identify the nearest waypoint that moves you closer to that goal, and in general terms, formulate a practical plan of how to get to each waypoint.

As you gather more information, make new connections, and gain experience, you will define a multitude of small objectives that will edge you closer to where you want to go. Those are what you write on the "notes" pages. Collectively and systematically achieving those micro-objectives will be what drives you to success.

Your Notes

## KEEP NOTES ... MAKE A LIST

When, as a teenager, I was trying to reach for my impossible dream, I used to carry a little notepad in my shirt pocket. When I learned something that might help me move toward my goal, I would note it in that book. When I found the name of someone in my destination industry, I noted it in my notebook. When I heard of someone doing big jobs—you got it—I noted it in my notebook.

After a while, I began to link things together. Questions began to occur to me. I flipped the note pad over and started to list my questions. That list got to be very long.

**When, each morning, I asked myself what I might do that day to get closer to my goal, I would refer to that list and those notes and most days an obvious (and fairly easy) option would jump out at me.**

Day by day, week by week, I got a little closer and a little closer. Sometimes I didn't know how close I was or how much further I had to go ... until I got there.

Your Notes

# 9

## MAINTAIN YOUR SENSE OF DIRECTION

Life is a journey. One that will take you through many hills and valleys, great highs and deep lows, before your journey ends.

There will be many varied events along the way to your goals, some you couldn't possibly foresee when you first set out. So be fluid enough to adapt your charted course to suit developing situations, or even change your proposed destination if a better one appears on the horizon.

What is important is to maintain a sense of direction, like following a compass toward ***today's*** micro-objective. Day by day, sometimes hour by hour, you edge toward your next proposed waypoint. Even if you have chosen to adjust your course, you need to maintain a sense of where you are going ***today***.

Without a sense of direction, you may just go around in circles.

Your Notes

# 10

## EACH MORNING, ASK YOURSELF, "WHAT WILL I DO TODAY TO GET ONE CENTIMETER CLOSER TO WHERE I'M TRYING TO GO?"

I am asked over and over again how I got into movies. Like there is some magic button that, when pressed, will somehow transport you to where you want to go. I explain that the secret to achieving anything is to analyze tiny steps that will get you closer to your dream and, every day, do a little something that edges you closer. It doesn't have to be a big thing. Maybe you search out some info on the Internet. Maybe you research the leaders in your field. Maybe you have a question and you search for an answer. But **don't let one day pass that you don't move yourself forward. Remember, it doesn't matter if you seem to be progressing slowly as long as you keep progressing**. Think like a marathon runner, not a sprinter. You have to put a lot of track behind you before you get invited to the Olympics.

When you wait until tomorrow, tomorrow becomes the day after. Then it's next week, and soon that attitude lets your dreams slip away. **If *every day* you move one centimeter closer to your goal, eventually you *must* get there.**

Your Notes

# 11

## NETWORK WITH EVERYBODY

Wherever you work or study, there's always a few people that you consider less than desirable. There's that nerdy guy that you think will go nowhere. There's that pushy girl that seems full of herself. There's that other guy that just tries too hard to be popular. None of them are on your list of people you want to invite to your house.

BUT ...

"Impossible to see, the future is." You never know where those guys might be in five years, what positions they might hold, and what opportunities they might be able to open for you. Even the most unlikely people sometimes get ahead of you, and it's the nerdy people who don't fit in that usually change the world.

**Make the most of every contact. Don't make enemies. Be friendly and useful. Network, network, network.**

## Your Notes

> *"So many people abandon their dreams and settle for something more mundane because society implies that it's 'sensible' to do so. Living a 'sensible' life may pay the bills, but what kind of stories does it generate for you to tell your grandkids in forty years?"*
>
> *— Nick Maley*

# 12

## "PRACTICAL LIMITS" ARE THE FIRST STEP TO ACCEPTING FAILURE

Not long ago, I was talking to a former school administrator about an "impossible dream" that I was pursuing. He asked me, "What practical limits have you put on this project?" I realized that what he really meant was: how long had I allowed myself to achieve my goals before accepting defeat? I think it was ***MIB*** star Will Smith who said that the problem with plan B is that it accepts that plan A might fail. It's hard enough to fight your way through everything life throws in your path without pre-arranging what you will do when you fail. So remember, practical limits stifle your potential, suppress your dreams, and smother your future.

This won't be popular with many parents, but when they insist on a safe back-up plan, it's because they have no faith that their child could actually achieve something exceptional. They fear their kid will fail to measure up to "normal" standards. Thus, they discourage the pursuit of lofty ambitions, insist on a plan B, and condemn their offspring to an average existence.

## Your Notes

*"If you settle for less, you get less."*

*— Nick Maley*

# 13

## IF YOU WANT TO GET A LOT OUT OF LIFE, YOU HAVE TO PUT A LOT IN

Okay. So, this is the page that will be unpopular with most of your friends. It's an unfortunate fact that to bake a good cake, you need to invest in good ingredients. You can't build anything if you have no tools. You can't become a famous rock guitarist if you don't learn to play the guitar and you can't become an Olympian without going to the gym. Worse still, when you finally get that big break, you need to prove your worth by putting in a bigger effort than the people around you.

In today's world, "hard work" and "perseverance" have become dirty words. Mostly from the mouths of under-achievers. **But you *must* put the effort in, or you have no chance of getting good results out.** And listening to friends who think it's cool to get away with doing as little as possible is the path to obscurity.

## Your Notes

# 14

## DON'T LET LIFE'S DIVERSIONS DERAIL YOU

So, you have a goal, and you have a list of things you need to do to get closer to that goal. You have faith in yourself, and you are determined to get a little closer to your dreams day by day. But your friends are having a party, and your favorite show is on TV. You need to go to the cellular office to get a new phone, and you need to go pay your electricity bill. You need to look for a new pair of shoes. You have to buy a present for your best friend's birthday, you need to go to the gym, and ... what was it you were going to do to get closer to achieving your dreams today?

Life is full of distractions. If you are not very careful, the day is eaten up by things that don't get you one iota closer to where you want to go.

**You *must* stay focused on what you need to do, or the lengthy journey that you need to undertake will become something you never fulfill.**

Your Notes

*"In the midst of problems and project deadlines it's difficult to de-stress and think clearly. Sit quietly, clear your mind and unwind."*
*— Nick Maley*

# 15

## DON'T GENERATE YOUR OWN DISTRACTIONS

As if the distractions life throws at us are not enough, you need to recognize the time-wasting things we do that distract ourselves.

- Arguing over things that can't be changed or issues that have no hope of a solution.
- Stressing over things that happened in the past.
- Debates with people whose perspective can't be changed.
- Trying to influence people who are convinced that they know everything.
- Spending time on anything that isn't moving you forward.
- Worrying about what other people think.
- Getting excited about things that could be better dealt with in a calm, methodical way.

The list could go on and on. But you get the idea. We are often our own worst distraction.

Your Notes

*"Think lateral, not linear. Better solutions are found by looking at a problem from a new perspective."*

*— Nick Maley*

# 16

## LOOK FOR A GUY WITH THE KEY TO THE BACK GATE

With the exclusion of a profession that requires college certification, such as a doctor or lawyer, **if there's an obvious route between you and where you want to go, *don't take it***. Don't knock on the studio gate and ask for George Lucas, James Cameron, or some other famous individual in your chosen field. If that route is obvious to you, it's obvious to two million other hopefuls. Someone is employed to take your information and say, "We'll call you if we need you."

In actuality, that prominent figurehead or famous individual that you want to work with isn't the person giving out jobs to people at your level. They hire someone, who hires someone else, who then hires someone else, who then hires someone like you. Learn who that last person is, where they are, and how you can get to know them on a less formal basis.

Being qualified just puts you on a long list of applicants. **Find someone doing all the best jobs. He has a key to the back gate and, when you carry his bag, you get those jobs, too.**

Your Notes

# 17

## KNOW YOUR INDUSTRY

This relates to the previous page. Whatever you want to do, if you want to gain access where others do not, it isn't enough to study the skills and techniques required to work in your industry. You need to study the industry itself.

What is the structure of personnel? Who within that hierarchy is in the position to hire a newbie like you? Who in that position is doing the most interesting jobs most frequently? How can you make contact with them? How can you shorten the odds to make it more likely that you can interact with that person? How can you get that person to notice you?

**Use any excuse to interact with people within your proposed industry at any level.** Take any job that gets you through the door to rub shoulders with others you can network with. That is a big step closer to your goal. You can't always move in a straight line. Flow through one opening to get past the obstacles and use your new contacts to flow back in the direction you want to go.

Your Notes

## THE OCEAN OF HUMANITY

Think of mankind as an ocean of people. Humanity drifts with the waves and currents that carry us all in a common direction.

First wave: you are born. Second wave: you go to school. Third wave: you get a girlfriend or boyfriend. Fourth wave: you go to college. Fifth wave: you go to work. Sixth wave: you get married. Seventh wave: you go to work again. Eighth wave: you have kids. Ninth wave: you go to work ***again***. Tenth wave: **you go to work a-g-a-i-n!**

You don't question where those waves are taking you because everyone you know is caught in the same current. Before you know it, you are in a rut of bills and other people's expectations, and there is no significant difference between your life and anyone else's.

**You can't swim against the current. But you can surf along the waves and end up on a different beach.** The other guys will think you are strange, maybe crazy. **But you don't get to live an exceptional life by doing what everyone else does.**

*"Never put off until tomorrow, what you can do today. Because if you do it today and you like it, you can do it all over again tomorrow."*

*— Arnold Schwarzenegger*

# ADOPTING THE RIGHT ATTITUDE

Your Notes

*"Before you start a project, give it the originality litmus test ... is your end product something you have never seen? Will it grab people's attention? Does it have a style all your own? If you can answer yes, yes, and yes, then you have found your originality."*

*— Nick Maley*

# 19

## YOU CAN'T LEAD BY FOLLOWING OTHERS

This is such a simple thought and such an obvious truth. But our instinct is to follow the herd. Going off in a different direction from everyone else often fills us with insecurity.

I was once talking to the Prime Minister of a Caribbean island who was suggesting a course of action that had proven popular on another island (St. Thomas). When I pointed out that doing the same would make his island a second-rate copy of St. Thomas whereas doing something different would make his island first-rate and original with a more unique product, he stared at me blankly. You can't be the red tree if you are copying your friends and neighbors.

Being the first person to attempt something in your area takes courage and imagination. You rarely succeed with your first attempt. That is okay. Adapt. Try again. It is better than following someone else who may be going down the path to mediocrity.

Your Notes

# 20

## YOU WON'T OVERCOME YOUR INSECURITIES UNLESS YOU FACE THEM

Fans often express surprise at the many diverse, creative things that I do. I am, or have been, a makeup artist, a prosthetics designer, a director of animatronics and creature effects, a screenwriter, a storyboard supervisor, an author, a poet, an artist/painter, a songwriter/composer, a curator, an entrepreneur, and a philanthropist. Basically, I have always grasped each task that I thought I could handle and, with self-confidence, a little planning, and a lot of determination, I have made the most of each endeavor.

I'm fortunate to have developed the methodology to figure out how to adapt my "tools" to do things I wasn't initially trained for. If you don't have enough courage to attempt something, then you can't reach the heights that activity might take you to. After all, **if you don't believe in yourself, nobody else will, either**.

**Don't let your fears hold you back.** Achieving something you didn't know you could is an awesome thrill.

Your Notes

# 21

## LIFE CAN BE A GREAT ADVENTURE ... IF YOU LET IT

There are so many influences in life that encourage us to "play it safe," not take risks, and put stability above the uncertainty of more glamorous possibilities. There is no doubt that it is more comfortable to be enveloped within the herd of humanity, moving through the stages of life with everyone else. It's more acceptable to the general populous to abide by the limitations considered "normal." But stretching beyond the norm, delving into the realms of uncertainty, also fires our adrenalin. Comfortable? Maybe not. Thrilling? Undoubtedly. Every endeavor may not result in success. **But while achievement brings satisfaction, setbacks provide experience.**

It's a matter of courage. If you like being one of the crowd, then stretching those boundaries is not for you. But if you are reading this book, then you are probably hoping for something more—and **a life of adventures awaits those with the courage to pursue their dreams.**

## Your Notes

# 22

## DON'T PUT YOURSELF IN A BOX

We are encouraged from an early age to decide what we want to be. A fireman? An engineer? A doctor? A lawyer? A graphic designer? A computer tech? Teenagers are asked that question time and again, pushing them toward a category thought to best fit their skills or learning ability.

**By all means, get qualified as something. But don't let that something define you.** If you study engineering, say you have an engineering degree. But don't call yourself an engineer because that confines you to a specific trade or profession. Maybe you will want to be a poet, too. Build upon the base you have established to expand your skills and combine new talents to open new horizons. This journey that we call "life" can be as diverse as your imagination allows. **Putting yourself in a box is the first step to limiting your expectations.** Maybe that's okay if you are only interested in paying the bills. But if you want a fulfilling life that takes you to places you could never have conceived when you began, keep your options and your mind open.

Your Notes

# 23

## BE DECISIVE

When faced with choices that might impact the rest of your life, it is easy to find yourself dithering on the brink of a conclusion, frozen in a state of indecision. Some people dither over what to have for breakfast and never make a decision over things of real importance. You will hear me say that opportunities won't wait for you to make up your mind. You need to weigh the possibilities, be decisive, and do it in a timely manner. Make a choice and don't look back to question what you did. Then make the most of the situation you find yourself in until the next opportunity arises to take you somewhere else.

As a leader, dithering will cause people to lose confidence in you. As a follower, being decisive will bring you greater opportunities. I am not telling you to jump without considering where you might land. Your risks should be calculated. But don't let indecision thwart your progress.

**While you dither over where you should be going, you are going nowhere.** It is better to be moving in a wrong direction than not to be moving at all, because once you are on the move you can always make a course adjustment.

Your Notes

# 24

## TALENT HELPS, BUT PERSISTENCE SUCCEEDS

It is normal in life to try something for a while and, when you don't experience immediate success, then decide to give up and hang with your friends instead. But **the only reason you can't do something is because you haven't practiced it long enough**. I was no better at painting than anyone else. But I wanted to be a better artist enough to invest eight hours a day for six months. In that relatively short time, the penny dropped and I figured out how to succeed at what I was doing. As a result, I earned thousands of $$$ from my artwork.

There are always people around you that seem more talented than you at whatever you are doing. But, when the going gets tough, **lazy, talented people fail as easily as lazy, untalented people. If you are struggling to keep up with them, when they give up, *you* are the one left standing.**

## Your Notes

> *"Color prejudice is just another symptom of herd or tribal thinking. Let's not forget that we are all the same color on the inside."*
>
> *— Nick Maley*

# 25

## DON'T HEED THE NAYSAYERS

It's easy to find reasons not to strive for something exceptional ...

- Friends will tell you it's too much effort.
- They will also tell you that it's smart to get by with the least amount of effort.
- Family will tell you there's too much risk of failure.
- Others will tell you your ambition is not practical and you should aim for something more easily achieved.
- Someone will tell you that you don't have the right skills.
- Another will say you don't know the right people.
- And a host of negative thinkers will say you are the wrong race, color, religion, or sex.

There are a million ways to give up before you start, but look to people who achieved greatness and the struggles they overcame and remember that **the only limitations that can stop your progress are the ones that you accept.**

## Your Notes

# 26

## BE A PADAWAN

So much emphasis is put on college. It's held to be the highest pinnacle of learning, so it's easy to overlook that cutting-edge people are so busy actually doing the job that they have no time to teach. Most professors are people who chose "teaching" because they couldn't make a living "doing." The point I am making is that you pay a small fortune to be taught by trailing-edge people, have little or no contact with your industry leaders, and start work weighed down by debt.

Often, I advise to "find a cutting edge person and offer to work for free." Sometimes, it is clear that the idea of working for free is not well-received. But you work without pay for years at college and end up with that big bill!

I am ***not*** putting down college. It is a good place to learn your basics and create a foundation upon which to build. But don't then go to a cutting-edge firm purporting to be an expert.

Instead say, "I studied the basics. Now I'm here to learn from the masters." A cutting-edge apprenticeship is worth much more than any college course.

Your Notes

# 27

## BUILD YOUR CAREER

Building a career is like building a house.

Your skills, your college qualifications, and your enthusiasm are only the foundation upon which you build: the things that make you employable on a basic level.

The contacts you then make, the industry research, the opportunities you grasp, things learned from your setbacks, your successful accomplishments, your growing reputation—all these are bricks that you stack on that basic foundation. You gather your bricks from whatever is available, and every new development is a block in your wall that you can take pride in. Your "house" will progress differently than your neighbor's. Don't fret about that. Just keep adding bricks until the walls are strong enough to support the "roof" as a figurehead in your industry.

Laying those bricks gave you the wisdom and experience for your "house" to withstand the winds of scrutiny and criticism. Don't rush to put a roof on your foundation too soon, or you run the risk of your house collapsing.

Your Notes

# 28

## STRETCH THE ENVELOPE, BUT DON'T BURST IT AT THE SEAMS

Sometimes our enthusiasm can get the better of our judgment. We all want to make a big leap. But moving steadily forward is often a wiser path. Firstly, build on what you know you can achieve. Secondly, add to that extended goals that you can reasonably predict to be achievable. Proceed with sure and steady steps. Big leaps involve higher risks, which could bring you to your knees and bruise more than your ego. **In short, don't let your enthusiasm write checks that your skills can't cash** and don't stretch yourself further than you can reach ... today (you'll reach further tomorrow).

When taking on new jobs, I used to visualize everything I ***hoped*** to achieve and promise the client the 70% I ***knew*** I could achieve. If I pushed the envelope enough to hit 85%, my client thought I was great for achieving 15% more. If I had promised 100%, he would have seen me as a 15% failure. **You will be measured by the expectations you generate.** Always strive for that distant goal. But keep expectations on the brink of what you can reasonably expect to reach within the schedule.

Your Notes

# 29

## PUT YOURSELF IN THE RIGHT PLACE AND WAIT FOR THE RIGHT TIME

It's no good preparing yourself for a chosen career and then sitting at home waiting for it to happen. Luck plays its part, but you must also shorten the odds. Study who can give you that opportunity. Assess where they are and aim to put yourself where you are most likely to be noticed.

That doesn't mean to put yourself in a place swamped with other hopefuls. That's the same as forming a queue. Any mass of hopefuls will be held at bay by the very people you are trying to attract. You need to be smarter than that.

Most of your competition won't study your chosen industry well enough to realize who can give you that opportunity. If a key person is hard to attain, find the main assistants close to those people. Be the exception. Target those individuals. Put yourself close to them and try to attract their attention. Be sure you are ready before you do this. You'll only get one opportunity, don't go off half-cocked.

## Your Notes

# 30

## YOU ONLY GET SOMETHING RIGHT BY BEING PERCEPTIVE ENOUGH TO SEE WHAT YOU DID THAT WAS WRONG

Whether you're painting a picture, crafting some item, writing a book, making a website, or building a business, your creative juices are at work. It's easy, when you are done, to let your pride and ego see your enterprise through rose-colored glasses. I encourage you to take pride in your achievements. But **if you can't look at your work and see what you could have done better, then you can't improve the next time**.

Improvement is the core that eventually makes someone great. So **the worst thing that can happen is that you think your creation is perfect. That is the end of your road to self-development**.

When other people think your work is fantastic, you need to still be self-critical enough to strive to make it better.

Your Notes

# 31

## DON'T LET YOUR OPPORTUNITIES DRIFT AWAY

I want you to think of your current life as a dock on the edge of a lake of infinite possibilities. Opportunities are like sailboats that occasionally drift by. You see that opportunity approaching. Maybe you question (or, more likely, fear) the uncertainty of leaping from the dock that you know onto that boat with no certainty of where you will be taken.

That opportunity does not tie itself to your dock. There is an optimum time when that opportunity is as close to you as it will get. Yes, there is always the chance that you will slip and fall into the water. But if you hesitate, once that optimum moment has passed, the opportunity begins to move away and it gets harder and harder to make the leap.

**Indecision is not your friend. Fear is your adversary. The traditional wisdom of playing it safe will leave you standing on that dock for the rest of your life** going nowhere.

Take the leap. **Every opportunity that passes is a door that has closed forever and an adventure that you will never know.**

## Your Notes

# 32

## THINK BIG … AND THEN THINK EVEN BIGGER

Someone in my museum said that as time goes by, it gets easier to settle for less. That's because you settle into accepting the same standards as the society around you and drifting along with everyone else. When they don't strive for something more, it seems more acceptable for you not to reach for something better, too.

Always remember what I said on the first page: another word for normal is average. But **if you shoot for the stars, even if you fall short, you might make it to the moon**.

Aim as high as you can imagine and, wherever you land, look up and try again for higher.

Your Notes

# 33

## KEEP A JOURNAL

Keeping a journal on your development and setbacks is not an essential step in reaching your goals, but I wish I had kept one. It will certainly help you write ***your*** book when the time comes (be sure to mention my encouragement and add your own). Notes make It's much easier to track your progress, look back on key events, or see what you are neglecting if you have a record of what you did and when.

When I was running the makeup effects foam latex lab on ***The Empire Strikes Back,*** I kept detailed notes on every adjustment I made to the mixtures, the temperature, the humidity, the time it took for the foam to gel, etc., and it was by cross referencing those notes that I knew what changes to make. You can do the same with your career; notes on who you met, where, and how; notes on things you learned or conclusions on what you need to learn. It may help you analyze what is working best for you and what is not. Notes at the end of the day will help you focus on fulfilling your destiny, just as reading this book does every morning.

Your Notes

> *"Every plan you make, every action that you contemplate, before you move ahead give a little thought to what reactions you might generate."*
> *— Nick Maley*

# 34

## THINK THE JOB THROUGH

When you have a specific project in mind, make a list of each stage of the project, then everything that you can envisage that you might need for each stage, then how long you can reasonably expect each stage or element to take to be completed. If you are thorough, then in this simple manner you form the basis of a plan, a schedule, and something to base a budget on.

Thinking the job through also often draws to your attention any elements not immediately in hand, areas where you might need assistance, a list of items that you will need along the way, and any gray areas that might need further research.

**Anticipating problems is the best way to avoid them.**

Approaching a job in a thorough manner is the best way to look efficient and inspire confidence.

Your Notes

# 35

## TO BE A "HIGH FLIER," YOU HAVE TO MAINTAIN A BALANCE BETWEEN LEAPING AND FALLING

- It takes energy to make that leap.
- It takes vision to know where you are leaping to.
- It takes faith, in yourself and in your purpose, to overcome the negativity that tries to keep you grounded.
- It takes courage to overcome your fear of falling.
- And it takes perception and adaptability to maintain your flight.

It's a difficult balance to maintain. Some people will say, "It's not worth the effort." Others will say, "There's too big a risk of failing." Those people never get to see the world from a higher altitude.

Isn't it a bigger risk to let life drift by without ever knowing if you could have reached your full potential?

Your Notes

# 36

## YOU CAN'T ACHIEVE WHAT YOU DON'T BELIEVE

People who achieve the impossible do so in part through vision and persistence. But at the core of accomplishing any goal is simply believing that it can be done.

Whenever you question your ability to perform a task or reach a goal, you make it that much harder to achieve. Many of the things I successfully completed were things I had never done before. I succeeded because I had confidence that (i) it could be done and (ii) I had a fair chance of being the one to do it. But as you will hear me say time and time again, fear, negativity, and doubt are your primary opponents. Self-doubt is the most defeatist influence of all. Because **if you don't believe you can achieve something, you won't**.

Most people accept failure before they even start. They don't undertake things that they think will take a lot of time or effort and justify that by the fact that their lack of effort is normal.

**The person who embraces his own self-doubt, defeats himself.**

Your Notes

# 37

## DON'T ACT YOUR AGE

If you are young: you need to act in an especially mature manner to overcome older people's expectation that young people are irresponsible and unreliable.

If you are old: you need to be extra active and innovative to overcome younger people's expectation that older people are slow and old-fashioned.

If you are young and want to live a rewarding life, ride on the enthusiasm of youth but absorb the wisdom of a mentor's experience.

If you are old and want to live a long life, don't sit in a chair and wait for something to happen. Get out there and make something happen.

If you are young and inexperienced, don't let that stop you from exploring all that the world has to offer.

If you are old and over-experienced, don't let old habits stop you exploring new horizons.

If you are in your middle years, GET OUT OF THAT RUT! Shake things up. Re-explore the enthusiasm of youth with all you learned so far.

## Your Notes

# 38

## SLEEP FASTER

Most people generally accept that they should get eight hours of sleep each night. That is the amount largely recommended in order to be alert and rested. When I was making movies, I often worked such long hours that I only slept five to six hours. I can't say that was ideal. Even so, I was able to effectively run a department and complete my assignments on schedule. Today, I generally sleep 7 hours and I want to explain why I'm sharing that gem of information with you.

If you sleep 8 hours a day and live 70 years, then you are sleeping ⅓ of your life: that's 300 months, or 25 years. Your waking life is 50 years. If you sleep 7 hours, you gain 365 hours of consciousness each year, 150 days every decade, 12.67 months every 25 years, and therefore 3 years, 2 months, and 7 hours of extra consciousness. That increases the length if your waking life by 6%.

Do you want to throw away those 3 extra years of experiences? Do you want to pass up 3 years of extra contacts, or lose 3 years of extra opportunities? If not ... as Arnold Schwarzenegger once said, "sleep faster!"

## Your Notes

# 39

## MAKE NO ASSUMPTIONS, UNLESS THEY ARE ABOUT YOURSELF

It seems like everyone does it. They make assumptions daily of what they expect that someone will do, or what they can presume will happen in a given situation. Those assumptions are based on the probable actions of average people in standard situations. But individuals have an uncanny knack of behaving illogically, and inspired leaders don't do what is predictable. **The most dangerous word in the English language is "presumably."** When you are trying to create something unique or are dealing with exceptional people or unusual situations, almost everything you assume or presume will be inaccurate. And when you are doing that on a tight schedule, **you can't afford the loss of time that your mistaken assumptions will consume.**

As Yoda would say, "You must unlearn what you have learned." Double-check the important details that your progress depends upon. Clearly define to others what you expect from them. **Don't end up with egg on your face and then blame someone else for not doing what YOU incorrectly anticipated.**

Your Notes

# 40

## FINISH THE JOB YOU STARTED

It's easy to allow repercussions of today's task to divert you to another job and not finish either. It's essential to stay focused on that initial assignment and not let your time be consumed by being sidetracked.

Let me offer a simple example. You bought something bulky and are making space for the delivery, a simple enough task. But you realize the only area big enough to accommodate the delivery is your closet. The closet is full of smaller stuff. So, you need to store the smaller stuff. You decide to buy containers to put the smaller stuff under the bed. As you drive to the store, you get a flat tire. Now you have to fix the tire to buy the boxes to move the small stuff to store the big stuff! You run out of time and the delivery is dumped outside in the rain.

**Stay focused** on the job you started. Do one job at a time. Move the small stuff to a temporary place. Complete the first job. Then move on to the second.

Deal with your problems one step at a time, or you will end up losing the day with nothing fully accomplished.

Your Notes

# 41

## YOU CAN'T STAY AHEAD OF THE PACK IF YOU DON'T KEEP MOVING FORWARD

This topic is directly related to being smart enough to see how to improve what you do. Yet it's also the key to maintaining a position as a leader in your field.

Once you have established yourself as a professional at the forefront of your subject—an expert—it is common to feel you have arrived at the destination you strove for. It's easy to implement your art using the same techniques that got you there. But other people are watching you. They aspire to copy what you have achieved. And if you don't develop further, eventually they catch up to you.

However old you are, however accomplished, "much to learn, you still have." So, **always strive to update your "tools" and develop yourself further. So while your competition is copying what you did yesterday, you stay ahead by carving out new territory for tomorrow.**

Your Notes

# 42

## STRIVE FOR THE BEST. LEARN FROM THE WORST

Every project you take on is a leap of faith as you work to turn nothing more than an idea into reality. Embrace them all 100%, big or small, and do the best you can to make each one as good as possible. Even the littlest job can open the door to something bigger. So **put every effort into all projects that you undertake**.

Unfortunately, not every project will be as successful as you hoped. Often your satisfaction is impeded by other people associated with the project or things beyond your control. Even when your plans don't produce the results you hoped for, you learn more about your craft. You learn more about yourself. You learn more about working with other people. And you learn one more way not to proceed.

It may be tough to take at the time. But **learning from your worst experiences will help you navigate your way to better ones**.

## Your Notes

# 43

## SETBACKS ARE OKAY

Following the thoughts of the last page, it's important to anticipate that the road to success will be littered with pitfalls and setbacks. Don't expect everything to go as planned. If you anticipate that problems will arise, you won't be disappointed when they do.

Success can be elusive. Don't measure yourself by how many problems interrupted your progress. **Measure yourself by how well you dealt with adversity. Measure yourself by how many times you picked yourself up again. Measure yourself by how you reset your course based on what you learned from that setback.**

Yoda was right to say, "the greatest teacher, failure is." But I would suggest that you term falling short of your aims as a setback—not as a failure. Your pride may be hurt. Your ego may be bruised. But setbacks are part of the journey of life. Success is still a possibility if you get back up and start again.

Your Notes

# 44

## YOU CAN'T MOVE FORWARD BY LOOKING BACKWARD

As I said before, life presents us with changing options and we are bound to make a few wrong decisions along the way. Think of those as life lessons that help you make better decisions in the future. But **don't dwell too long on events from the past. Don't keep thinking of what might have been.** Because **as long as you are looking backward, you restrict yourself from moving forward**.

Focusing too much on what you lost or where you have been limits your ability to see the next opportunity approaching.

Move on with life and make the most of what is yet to come.

Your Notes

*"Even if everyone you know is living on credit and running up debts that in future will limit their options doesn't mean you have to do that, too."*

*— Nick Maley*

# 45

## WORK WITHIN YOUR BUDGET. STAY WITHIN YOUR MEANS

We live in a world where running up big debts in order to get ahead is considered normal. In the States, everyone seems to accept that students start their working lives with extensive debts. Your credit rating gets its importance on the basis that it is normal for most citizens to live on borrowed money. An accepted part of starting a business is borrowing capital. It isn't uncommon for people to leverage or liquidate the equity from one loan to secure another. But just because that is what others do, doesn't mean you have to do it, too. We start these projects with the best of intentions, but things don't always go the way we hoped. Nothing ends a dream as quickly as bills you can't pay. **It's critically important that you don't let your optimism encourage you to bite off more debt than you can chew.** It's better to start small and grow with your profits than start big then crash and burn. Base your budgets on minimum financial expectation, not on average or maximized projections. Ensure your overhead doesn't outweigh your income at times when business is slow. **Debts limit your options, and financial stress negatively dictates your actions.**

Your Notes

# 46

## LET SIMPLICITY BE THE BASIS OF YOUR GENIUS

The problem with inventing something new is that you have to pay the production costs and develop support facilities for your invention. Of course, people will like it because it is new and does something otherwise unseen. But you can acquire that kudos without paying those production costs if you base your creation on things already commonly available. Just adapt them into something that ***appears*** to be unique. By doing that, your production costs plummet. Getting spares is easy. But best of all, the products you adapt are already tried and tested, so reliability of your invention skyrockets.

**The trick is to look at everyday items with a new eye.** Study the basics of what makes them work, what their shapes inspire in your imagination, how you could use them to create something new. Keep those things in mind when others set you new projects. But let your clients think you created something ***new*** in record time.

Your Notes

# 47

## WHY PAY FOR SOMEONE ELSE'S MISTAKES WHEN YOU GET YOUR OWN MISTAKES FOR FREE?

It can be infuriating to pay someone to do a job, tell them exactly what you want, then have them do something that doesn't entirely suit your purpose and give you excuses why it had to be that way. Being an independent thinker who visualizes alternative ways of doing things, it's frustrating to employ someone who insists on doing things the standard way rather than adapting their skill and knowledge to achieve what you asked for.

So when you have a job you don't know how to do, ***watch what the specialist does***. Learn that new skill and next time, maybe try doing it yourself. **Just because you have never done something before is no reason not to attempt it**. Doing so saves you money, expands your abilities, and leads you to unexpected horizons. That's at the heart of personal development.

Don't apply this principle to the electrics in your house, perform surgery on your sister, or to anything that could be dangerous to you or other people.

Your Notes

# 48

## TEMPER YOUR DREAMS WITH PRACTICAL EXPECTATIONS

This sounds like a contradiction to other things I said—but really, it is not.

There is no point in embarking on your journey with starry eyes and impractical expectations. You won't achieve your goals with wishful thinking or blind optimism. That just leads you into situations you aren't prepared for. **Anticipate potential obstacles on the hard road ahead. Then you aren't surprised or derailed when the going gets tough.** Know your industry. Learn what to expect. Don't think you will find instant success. Listen to people who walked that path before you. Note the pitfalls they share with you. That is the best way to avoid them.

**The road to success is aided by a realistic understanding of the problems you will have to navigate.** If you are prepared for them, it is easier to take them in your stride.

## Your Notes

*"People who rise through the ranks understand better the complexities of the job they manage and the emotions or ambitions of those people who assist them. In essence, you'll be better at the top if you rose from the bottom."*

*— Nick Maley*

# 49

## YOU CAN'T SOAR AMONGST THE STARS WHILE HOLDING OTHER PEOPLE DOWN

However good you are at whatever you do, there's going to come a time when you need a team of helpers. The better your team is, the better you look. But some bosses believe that they can only stay on top by holding down the people beneath them. **While you're busy suppressing your team, you aren't free to be the best *you* can be.** Remember, "Fear of loss is a path to the Dark Side." You don't develop loyalty that way, and a team doesn't do their best work for a boss that they resent. None of that helps your career.

So, don't worry about training your competition. "Pass on what you have learned." Build on your joint ideas and remain the figurehead while **uplifting the team around you**. Focus on their strengths and work around their weaknesses. Develop their special skills. Give them pride in their achievements. **Aid their journey toward exceptional lives and they will carry you with them.** Your team will love you for it and, free of interdepartmental politics, your ideas will be more innovative. **That's how you develop a winning team and teams that win usually stick together.**

Your Notes

# 50

## WHAT IS "SUCCESS?"

The average person measures success by how much money someone earns and how big their possessions are. Some measure it by fame. But the scale by which success should really be measured is by how much satisfaction you gain from your level of achievement.

**If you can live your life doing what you enjoy, that, in itself, is a huge success!**

If you love the work you do, then going to work is a joy. And that, too, is a success.

**The pile of money you have in the bank means nothing if you have no real satisfaction in what you do.** How many famous people kill themselves because fame and fortune didn't bring them the satisfaction they desired?

**If you can achieve consistent satisfaction, you are rich beyond measure.**

# 51

## THE LIGHT AND THE DARK

George Lucas once said that ***Star Wars*** is a struggle between two types of people: compassionate people vs. selfish people. That is the essence of the classic trilogy. Light against dark. Good against evil. At its root is a philosophy that runs through most religions: doing the right thing, caring for others, doing the least harm, and being one with "the Force"—whichever "force" you believe in. Yes, there is plenty of action and adventure, too. But stormtroopers, X-wings, and TIE fighters are just the dressing on a story of imperfect, good-hearted humans (a mouthy princess, a reluctant hero, and a kid who thinks he knows everything) fighting the oppression of aggressive, selfish, bad people. The dark side is seductive. The reward for being bad is more immediate. It's too easy to say, "I'm a Vader fan." (And many people tell me just that.) But it's not okay to kill all the padawans, even if later you say you are sorry. Hitler was probably sorry before he shot himself. That doesn't mean it okay to kill six-million people.

When Yoda said, "Luminous beings are we ..." what do you think he meant? To me, that is clearly a reference to the "light side." But beyond the obvious reference to good and bad, perhaps we should also apply that to other "light and dark" attributes that can influence our road to success: optimistic and pessimistic, upbeat and downbeat, encouraging and discouraging.

If you are a newbie trying to join a leading team, ask yourself, who wants a teammate who is pessimistic and discouraging? If you are trying to build a winning team, ask yourself, who wants to work for a boss who is downbeat or negative? And nobody likes a teammate or boss who is selfish.

The message is simple. Want to succeed? Be a luminous being! Radiate positive energy. Celebrate what is half full. Don't dwell on what's half empty. Do the right thing for your friends, colleagues, and even strangers. Sometimes it seems to go against your interests. But in the long run, being part of the light, the solution, will bring you greater rewards than being part of the problem.

*"It's easier to be wise in the calm of the evening than it is to follow that wisdom through the stress of the day. Take a moment to feel* ***your*** *force and be the Master of your anxiety."*

*— Nick Maley*

# DEALING WITH LIFE

## Your Notes

*"When your head swims, you make rash decisions, so finding solutions is much harder. Take a moment to sit down and let your emotions settle."*

*— Nick Maley*

# 52

## YOU CAN'T CONTROL CIRCUMSTANCES. YOU CAN ONLY CONTROL YOUR REACTION TO THEM

I owe a lot to my father, who taught me how to deal with stressful situations when you don't have the means to alter them.

When I was still quite small, he explained to me that **it is hard enough to deal with things that you *can* change without stressing over things that you can't**. Allowing things that can't be altered to disrupt what you need to do means you not only suffer the initial stress, but also the stress of the consequences. You are allowing a chain reaction to get underway that escalates your anxiety and diminishes your ability to deal with things in a practical manner.

The problem is that we usually react to situations instinctively, and **instinctive reactions, in business and personal relationships, almost always result in unwise decisions and actions**.

When things are going wrong, don't panic. Take a moment, make a plan on how best to deal with the situation (or buy yourself time to figure out a plan), then ***act*** on that plan. **Don't REACT. Pause, plan, and ACT.**

## Your Notes

# 53

## NEGATIVITY IS INFECTIOUS. BEWARE OF UNWARRANTED EPIDEMICS

Dealing with negativity is ***such*** an important part of achieving your goals, because negativity is all around us. Attitudes, generally, are infectious—none more so than negativity. In fact, when it comes to striving for anything beyond the norm, the standards adopted by society are intrinsically defeatist and anything beyond "normal" is considered risky.

People who accept normal expectations consider those of us who strive for more as strange or even delusional. If the neighbors think reaching for your dreams is risky, then probably your family does, too. Society considers that striving for a conventional "professional" career is the highest accolade. But being a lawyer or accountant or doctor just puts you in a new pool of associates where the "average" is higher. If you strive for more, expect to experience discouragement.

The point is that **negativity is an epidemic that surrounds you. Brace yourself for that onslaught or you have no hope of reaching your dreams.**

## Your Notes

# 54

## MONEY FUELS LIFE, BUT YOU ONLY NEED ENOUGH FUEL TO GET WHERE YOU WANT TO GO

We live in a materialistic society that encourages us to measure success by financial wealth and judge individuals by the size of their possessions. But someone who loves what they do is more successful than a wealthy individual who sacrifices his or her principles and personal relationships to pursue profit.

Whilst agreeing that money isn't everything, I have to admit that poverty isn't anything. We ***do*** need enough money to fuel the lives we live. **But using your time in the pursuit of more than you need is a worthless waste of your life!** Make enough money to live the life you want. Put a little buffer away for unforeseen circumstances. Don't let the pursuit of money restrict your horizons or limit the life experiences needed to grow as a caring human being. **We are the sum of our experiences, and limiting those experiences by devoting our time to acquiring excess money we will never use limits true growth.**

In short, **make money to live. Don't live to make money.**

Your Notes

# 55

## BEWARE OF MISCONCEPTIONS MASQUERADING AS THE TRUTH

Remember that party game where you whisper something in someone's ear that they pass around in a circle? Remember how it was misrepresented by the time it got back to you? Generally speaking, most things you hear/read are equally distorted.

Commonly, **something that is partly true gets passed on as if it is the whole truth**. Someone else interprets what they read and tells a friend (or tweets) a less-well-defined version of what they presume from what they read. As the information is passed along, it gets condensed and shortened and that distortion often becomes commonly accepted as the "truth."

**Over time, myth and misinformation gain credence over actual facts. The truth becomes more elusive than the popular misconception. Eventually, accuracy is lost with the passing of those who actually witnessed the events.**

Just because something is common knowledge, don't take it as gospel. For important issues, double check your "facts" with an irrefutable source.

Your Notes

*"At first they will think you are a 'flake' for trying to achieve something beyond the norm. Then, one day, they ask for your autograph."*
—*Nick Maley*

# 56

## NO PAIN, NO GAIN

Sometimes it will feel like nothing is going right; especially when you suffer a series of disappointments or multiple setbacks of some kind. But that is all part of the journey to success.

Overcoming setbacks makes you stronger. It is like pumping up muscles through exercise. You are pumping up your knowledge base through gaining experience. Learning what doesn't work leads you to what does. The mental process of eliminating possibilities identifies the solution.

You will hear me stress in many ways that nobody said this journey would be easy. It is not an original thought. But it is nonetheless true that if it were easy, then everyone would be doing it.

**Persevering through adversity to a satisfactory conclusion is what will make others describe you as exceptional.**

Your Notes

# 57

## THE SIDEKICK SHARES THE ADVENTURE ... WHILE THE PRINCIPLE TAKES THE STRESS

When you join a creative team, it's natural to want to have a more important role. You start as the new guy, making coffee and doing the drudgery. When you get to be a junior, actually doing stuff, you long for a more senior role. When you get that post, you envy the second-in-command in the department who is dealing with much of the best work. And when you have that job, you wonder why the head guy does some of the things he does and long to take control of everything.

But once you have that top position, suddenly you are dealing with politics, personalities, schedules, and budgets. You don't have time to do the stuff you thought you would. Many of the best jobs go to your second-in-command. You have to make compromises you didn't foresee. You have the stress of struggling to get your team to achieve what you could have done yourself. And the people above you keep pressing for more and more, in less time.

**The second-in-command may be the sidekick with a little less glory, but he or she has a lot more fun and sleeps better at night.**

Your Notes

# "RETIREMENT" IS A DIRTY WORD

When starting out on your chosen path, retirement is not the first consideration on your mind. But let's take a moment to consider society's precept of a working life.

Traditional wisdom subscribes that:

i. You to go to school.
ii. You work hard.
iii. You get a good job.
iv. You work for forty years.
v. You retire.
vi. You sit in a chair and wait to die.

Doesn't seem too appealing to me.

A large part of what keeps us young and active are our daily goals and activities. You need a good reason to get up every day. You need to have constant stimulation for your brain and body because if you don't use it, you lose it. So I propose that we retire the word "retirement." **Think more in terms of "a new beginning" to revitalize life by opening a new chapter, with new goals and new experiences that make the most of the skills and understanding that you gained on your life's journey.**

*"Compassion is cool. Encouragement costs you nothing and it opens the door for new alliances."*

*— Nick Maley*

# HUMAN RELATIONS

Your Notes

# 59

## STRIVING FOR AN EXCEPTIONAL LIFE? YOU NEED TO CHOOSE AN EXCEPTIONAL WIFE (OR HUBBY)

As if it isn't hard enough to follow your dreams, finding a partner to share that journey makes things even more complex. Few of us control who we find attractive and opposites really ***can*** attract. If you pursue an adventurous career and you hitch yourself to someone reserved or doubtful, at some point you'll have to choose twixt your lover and your dreams. Aspirations are often consumed by "practical choices" made to support the family or put food on the table. If you want to succeed in a freelance world, you have to be largely married to your career.

There is no easy solution here. But for starters, if possible, when you first get involved with someone, ask yourself if their outlook on life matches yours. If it doesn't, think carefully before risking heartache. Much of this can be avoided if you choose a partner from within your chosen industry who shares your aspirations and your goals. Otherwise, establish your place in the world before getting "serious" with anyone. You need to share your life with someone who supports your madness. Not someone thinks you should be normal.

Your Notes

# 60

## COMMITTEES STIFLE INSPIRED IDEAS

The exaltation of democracy has encouraged the belief that group decisions are more valuable than the ideas of the individual. But the very nature of group decisions averages out the most inspired suggestions with the most inane. That generally results in decisions and actions that are largely average.

Almost without exception, innovative concepts have been championed by individuals who become figureheads for their enterprise. **Great ideas are created by spirited individuals with unusual vision. Such originality is defused by committees who are obliged to accommodate the least-inspired member of their team.**

The exception is perhaps a "think tank" of like-minded individuals, already exceptional in their field. But usually there is a leader who makes decisions based on the suggestions of his team members.

**Generally, if at all possible, avoid getting strung up in making decisions by committee. At best they delay your progress. At worst they stifle creativity.**

Your Notes

# 61

## WHEN YOU ARE SENSITIVE ON THE INSIDE, YOU NEED TO BE TOUGH ON THE OUTSIDE

Most truly creative people are also very sensitive. To be perceptive enough to see what others do not, our senses need to be more receptive than theirs. But our drive to be creative puts us in the forefront where the spotlight can be intimidating and criticism can be harsh.

I can't say that I am always good at hiding my emotions. I am not. But, to get through some of those tough high-profile situations, you need to try to hold your sensitivity inside and put a strong face forward. When people want to be critical, just don't take it on. **Don't let their negativity undermine your vision or shake your confidence.** Put on a brave face, follow your instinct, and lick your wounds in private.

## Your Notes

# 62

## DON'T RISE TO AGGRESSION

When other people get aggressive, it's so easy to let your temper rise with theirs. That is especially true if you are already frustrated by trying to solve some other problem. But letting tempers flare doesn't help anything. **Allowing yourself to be drawn into an argument just distracts you from what you are trying to achieve.**

Maybe that other person is having a bad day. But don't let your day be ruined by theirs. Don't let yourself be distracted from the things you need to achieve today by someone whose mindset you probably can't change anyway.

When you meet aggression, diffuse the situation by saying nothing or acquiescing, or simply walking away. Whatever you do, don't enter the argument. It just wastes your time. Even explaining yourself can inflame tempers and probably won't improve anything.

Your Notes

# 63

## DON'T BE BLINDED BY BITTERNESS

I mentioned that things don't always go the way we want. Unexpected events may block our path. Other people's actions or opinions may hinder progress. Their jealousy or spiteful acts might be designed specifically to aid their own agenda while obstructing yours. Sometimes an important opportunity may slip away, and you wonder if another will ever come your way.

I have said before that your journey will be fraught with hurdles and that worrying about past acts won't help you seize the next big break. But the worst reaction you can have is to let outside influences generate bitterness within you. **Bitterness warps your perception.** It gets in the way of seeing the route to your next opportunity. It eats at your insides and distracts you from moving ahead efficiently. Bitterness, like hate, leads to the dark side. Shake it off. **Fretting doesn't help.** Pity those wretches who have to resort to negative tactics. Learn from delays and mistakes and focus more on what you need to do and where you need to go.

Your Notes

# 64

## LET YOUR PARTNER BE WHO THEY WANT TO BE

My wife and I have weathered our partnership for over forty years. Of course we have had a few disagreements in that time, but largely we have found a formula for longevity. We live together. We work together. But we don't get tired of each other and we don't feel our personal freedoms are restricted by the other.

**The number one most important element of a lasting relationship is to give your life partner the room to be who *they* want to be, and not try to change them into the person *you* think they should be.** If you choose the latter course, your partner feels obliged to pretend to be who you want while they secretly do what they long to do. That builds invisible walls and can even drive your lover away. **Support each other's insane interests, or you'll end up with nothing in common.**

The second most important element is frank communication. When things are going astray, calmly, quietly talk about it.

Lastly: **If you treat your partner like a child, don't be surprised if they act like one.**

# 65

## TAKE PRIDE IN BEING "DIFFERENT"

Deep down in our hearts, we all want to fit in; we all want to be popular and accepted by our peers. So often we think there must be something wrong with us when we are the odd one out: different, geeky, not embraced by the "in" crowd. If you are sensitive, or less than attractive, or challenged in some way, being ostracized or made fun of can be heartbreaking.

Well, screw that.

The world is changed by people who are "different," so how can it be a bad thing? Geeks created Apple and Microsoft. Nerds founded Google and Yahoo. Great artists in any field are distinctly "different" and overcoming "special needs" often reveals talents nobody ever expected. Look at Yoda. Do you think he worries about being different when he says, "Judge me by my size, do you?"

Anyone who is exceptional at anything can't possibly be the same as everyone else. That is why we call them **exceptional**. Don't worry about what other people think. Go change the world.

That said, of course it's extremely difficult to celebrate being different if you face challenges like autism, Down syndrome, attention deficit, or even dyslexia. People, especially kids, can be cruel to others who are "different." Well, remember what I said about normal people being average and ordinary? Just because you are different, doesn't make you any less important. It doesn't make you less talented in your own unique way. Don't focus on your weaknesses, focus on your strengths. You should feel sorry for people who are so bigoted that they think being normal is a good thing. The extraordinary people who battle special challenges every day should take particular pride in their achievements because every day, their struggle makes them stronger. Every day, they overcome difficulties regular folk never have to address. And often, they develop exceptional skills that are way beyond "normal."

As a youngster, I was underrated for being dyslexic, with a degree of attention deficit, too. Look at me. I did okay. And you can, too, if you don't let other people's small-minded views limit your perception of your own self-worth and the possibilities life has in store for you.

*"For the next generation, the greatest challenge to living beyond the norm is going to be computer processing. Never before have we had a society so heavily monitored and controlled by automated systems designed to manage average citizens."*

*—Nick Maley*

# REALITIES OF THE DIGITAL DOMAIN

Your Notes

# 66

## YOU CAN'T NEGOTIATE WITH A COMPUTER SYSTEM

Computers are taking over the structure of our lives. They dictate what we can do online, how our money is controlled, what other people know about us, and what we have access to. More and more, we are confronted by computer systems that block our path or require us to invest time dealing with their system just to access what we need.

**Computers have no respect for the value of your time.** They only care about what they were programmed to do, and their actions are limited by the lack of foresight of their programmers.

As all these systems are being put in place, the value of dealing with a human being becomes clearer and rarer. Learn what you can from the computer, but then connect with a human. You can't negotiate with a computer or even ask a question if the answer isn't preprogrammed into the system.

Basing your creativity on a program someone else created limits your results to whatever the programmer designed it to do.

Your Notes

> *"Don't let your devices distract from your real-time relationships or you may find you don't have any."*
>
> *— Nick Maley*

# 67

## USE THE INTERNET AS A TOOL— NOT A PASTIME

These days, most people walk around with the Internet on their hip or in their bag. They are always connected to what's new; to friends, family, associates, and the world, with quick access to answers to questions, resources, suppliers, and instruction videos. In many ways, it is so much easier to access tools and resources that help you achieve your goals. But at the same time, there is so much to distract you from them, too.

When the Internet began to take hold in the mid-nineties, nobody could ever have guessed the invention of YouTube, Instagram, Facebook, Twitter, and other addictive social media. As interesting as playing games; watching what other people are doing; and sharing comments, rumors, and various pages might be; **the Internet has become the biggest distraction of all time**.

To achieve your goals, you need to analyze your use of the net and see how productive your use of time is. Check your notes and use the net to achieve ***today's*** goals, rather than waste the day on things that don't move you toward your dreams.

## Your Notes

## BEWARE OF AVERAGE OPINIONS

There was a time when the populous believed that the world was flat. Being a generally held belief did not make that accurate. The same thing goes today for thousands of opinions on the Internet, where opinions are expressed by average individuals rather than knowledgeable experts. Just because a million people like something, doesn't make it especially smart, true, or advantageous.

The phenomenon of something going viral on the net, and the notoriety it brings to whoever posted it, encourages viewers to emulate that person and exalt that idea. **Does adopting the attitudes of a million other people make you stand out from the crowd? No. It doesn't.** Can you create something original by emulating what someone else already did? Of course not.

Social media popularizes average beliefs. You won't find success by emulating the opinions of the masses.

Your Notes

"*Computers and other devises are seductive. They lure us with spectacular games, online tools, mobile phones, and social media. As we embrace them they undermine our privacy, they erode our independence, and quietly negate centuries of personal freedoms.*"

—*Nick Maley*

## A COMMENT

**As the digital age invades every aspect of our lives, computers control ...**

- Phone and online access to your bank.
- Use of your credit card.
- Your liquid assets (your money is really just a credit in a computer).
- Your education.
- Bureaucratic forms of all kinds.
- Passport application, airline travel, and international immigration.
- Access to the Internet and the Internet itself.
- Online shopping and services.
- Your driving license.
- And much more than I can list here.

Cell phones track where you are. Credit cards track what you spend. Browsers track what you watch and what you buy. I remember when it was considered an unacceptable invasion of privacy to tap a phone. Now it is "'normal"' for voice and text messages to be scanned by computers to pick up keywords that indicate whether or not you are unacceptable to society. How long will it be before it is "normal" for your computer to watch you while you surf the net, work, and play?

*"Your success is largely dependent upon how you deal with your disasters."*

*—Nick Maley*

# HARSH REALITIES

## Your Notes

> *"They say that in our dying moments, our life will flash before our eyes. It will be up to you whether or not yours is worth watching."*
>
> *— Anonymous*

# 69

## YOU CAN'T LIVE AN EXCEPTIONAL LIFE WITHOUT MAKING AN EXCEPTIONAL EFFORT

I'm sorry to be the one to tell you this but, unless you were born into a rich family, you get out of life what you put in. **If you can't be bothered to make the effort to be exceptional, there's virtually no chance that it will happen on its own, or by accident.**

It's almost certain that every one of your heroes lives an exceptional life. And they did not get there by sitting on a couch watching TV or playing video games. Astronauts, not normal. Olympians, not normal. Pop stars, not normal. Movie stars, not normal. Entrepreneurs, not normal. They all had to make an exceptional effort to train for their career OR learn their craft and struggle against the odds to find recognition.

Yes, it's going to be hard. Yes, it might take ten years to achieve your goal. But do you want to be ninety asking yourself why you spent fifty years doing something you didn't want to do?

**You will be whatever you make of yourself, or you will only have yourself to blame for whatever you allowed yourself to become.**

## Your Notes

> *"Many of the world's problems could be resolved if we just had respect for each other's beliefs, thought processes, and traditions."*
>
> *— Nick Maley*

# 70

## NO MATTER WHAT YOU SAY, PEOPLE WILL REMEMBER YOU FOR WHAT YOU DO

I'm probably not the first person to tell you that your actions speak for you. That doesn't make it any less true. You need to ensure that your actions live up to your words.

**Actions are the biggest telltale of who you truly are. Words only indicate what you want others to *think* you are.** If your actions match what you said, people will respect you for being reliable. If your actions don't match what you said, they won't have faith in you next time.

Make every day count. Respect your commitments, personal and contractual. Do everything possible to stay on schedule and on budget. Keep your promises. Because valued contacts are hard to establish and they never forget when someone lets them down.

Your Notes

# 71

## IF YOU HAVE TO WORK JUST TO MAINTAIN YOUR POSSESSIONS, YOU DON'T REALLY OWN THAT STUFF. IT OWNS YOU

TV commercials and shows popularize big houses and expensive belongings. People work hard to acquire these things, thinking that other people will respect them for what they possess. But the truth is that most people resent you for having things they don't. They begrudge you having that fancy car. Some want to scratch it up for you. They think it's okay to steal from you because you have so much more than they do.

As a result, you spend more money to protect your stuff, maybe hiring people to look after it and paying high bills to maintain it. **You've created a money-go-round where you have to work harder just to maintain the things you have.** You are working for your stuff. You don't own it. It owns you.

**Being satisfied to live a simpler life means people are less jealous of you, your stress diminishes, you have more time for loved ones, more time to experience the richness that life has to offer, and more time to achieve something extraordinary.**

Your Notes

# 72

## ACTING AND SCREENWRITING: EXERCISES IN REJECTION

*(skip this page if it doesn't relate to you)*

Hopefully, you already read the page about having practical expectations. Well, of all the things you can hope to do, the areas in which you are most likely to encounter constant rejection are scriptwriting and acting.

Every time an actor goes for an audition, chances are that there are 200 other actors there for the same part. You need to develop a thick skin and have an ego big enough to keep smiling despite frequent disappointment.

Script writers face a different problem. People with the money to make movies have preconceived ideas of what they want to make. No matter how brilliant your ideas are, if they don't fit with their interests, your script doesn't get read. If it ***is*** similar to their interests, they fear you will claim they stole your ideas and still don't read it. **Most successful scriptwriters are given a short synopsis and develop other people's concepts.** You have more leverage if you have written a successful novel first.

I am not saying don't pursue these careers. I'm just trying to prepare you for having practical expectations.

Your Notes

# 73

## WHEN THE JOURNEY BRINGS YOU DOWN ...

Your journey toward a rewarding existence will take you through many emotions. You need to be focused and determined to get through the daily barrage of negativity in order to develop the person you are destined to become. There will be highlights and personal triumphs. But there will also be dark valleys where the struggle gives way to depression, when that tenuous goal seems unattainable, and self-doubt invades your endeavors.

It is for those days that I wrote this book. Read a page or two and let that lift you enough to keep you going just one more day.

Then do the same thing tomorrow.

When I was really down, I used to think about what it would be like to go tell the naysayers that they were right all along, that I had wasted the effort and finally failed. That always kept me going a little further.

*"I'm hoping my words will help a new generation of creative minds traverse the rocky road to self-fulfillment, but striving for an exceptional life is never easy, and they need to stick at it day after day to reach their destiny. The people who fall by the wayside will never know the taste of true satisfaction."*

*— Nick Maley*

# FINAL THOUGHTS

Your Notes

# 74

## BE THE RIVER THAT FLOWS TO THE SEA

To help you with the constant challenges that you will meet on the journey toward your life goals, **I want you to think of yourself as a river and your ultimate goal as the sea that you are destined to reach.**

On that journey, the river meets many obstacles. As it grows from a brook into a stream, it might have enough momentum to sweep aside the smaller boulders. But when it faces a big obstruction, even a river doesn't have the strength to move a mountain. Does it say "this is too big" and give up? No. Instead, it adjusts its path. It finds a way ***around*** the obstacle. It is not a highway. It does not waste its resources trying to continue in a straight line. It saves its energy as it weaves and wanders to find a new path to its destination.

**Whatever gets in its way, the river *will* eventually always reach the sea.**

Your Notes

# 75

## DON'T LET THE PERSON YOU ARE DESTINED TO BECOME BE SMOTHERED BY THE INSECURITIES OF WHO YOU ARE NOW

I have said it several times: it is normal to be filled with doubts and fears, especially when you set out to achieve something beyond usual.

It is normal to wonder if you have the stamina to climb the mountain you have set for yourself. It is normal to question your direction when all your friends are headed somewhere else. It is normal to feel the influence of other people's negativity.

You know what I think of "normal."

Swallow your insecurities, step up to the plate, and take your best shot. And if you fall on your face, get up and try again. Remember, **when Luke said, "I don't believe it," Yoda responded, "That is why you fail."**

**If you don't believe in yourself, you can be certain that nobody else will. If you don't have the courage to stand out in the crowd, you will be lost in the herd.**

Your Notes

# 76

## THE PEOPLE WHO FAIL ARE THOSE WHO GIVE UP

This is going to be a very short page, but a very important one because it reinforces everything I say in this book.

No matter how hard the going gets, stay focused on where you are headed, edge a little closer every day, and **don't give up**.

Remember: **you can achieve anything if you stick at it long enough to make it happen**. Your journey will be full of obstacles and setbacks. But **just because you haven't succeeded (yet), that does not mean you have failed**.

**You haven't failed until you have given up.**

## Your Notes

# 77

## ONE LAST THOUGHT ...

When you are young, time seems so unimportant. There's lots of it ... every day. And you seem to have to wait forever to become an adult. But not long after that, you start to suspect that time is passing faster. All too soon you are thirty, then forty, and not so long after that you begin to realize that your life is actually ebbing away.

**The cruel truth is that every day that you waste or allow yourself to be distracted by other things is actually a little piece of your life that you can never get back.** Every time you put something off until tomorrow, you let your life goals slip farther away.

Eternity will not remember you for all the games you played. Nobody will remember you for all the TV shows you watched. Even your Facebook "friends" will not remember you for all the social media that you posted. Do you really want your life to be measured by all your wasted moments? **Because history will never remember you for all the things you never did.**

Those were your 77 steps. If you read every day, eleven weeks have passed since you started. Now you can either read the following section on how I used these principles to achieve my dreams or you can start afresh at "Core Principles" again. This time read your notes, too, and see how many things you wrote that you failed to complete these last few months. Delete the things that you achieved and prioritize the things you have yet to do.

If you made a lot of progress, be proud. If you didn't, you know you need to concentrate harder or you will never realize your dreams. If you don't make the effort to change your life, nobody else can do it for you.

Whichever you choose, don't finish by putting this book on a shelf. Not unless you are settling for an average existence. Focus on that "future you." Continue to read a page ***each day*** and strive to meet the person you are destined to become.

# A LIFE BEYOND THE BOX

## APPLYING THOSE PRINCIPLES

## FOR THOSE OF YOU WHO DON'T BELIEVE A MAN CAN FLY …

When I was ten years old, we finally moved out of the room my parents inhabited in my grandma's rented house and moved into a council flat. My mother cried. She was ***so*** happy to have her own apartment in that low-income housing estate.

My dad was an actor and singer, struggling to get enough work to pay the bills. Some people would say he was a failure because we were poor, but he lived his dream until the day he died. In my eyes, that makes him a success.

In fact, my dad worked a lot. But production companies considered that supporting actors were a dime a dozen. For every job, there were 300 applicants auditioning, and the nature of supply and demand resulted in lesser-known performers not being paid well. But year after year, he sang and did voice-overs for ice shows in the winter, cabaret at theaters

My dad was a creative spirit who fired my imagination

on seaside piers through the summer, and periodically small parts in musicals playing in the West End of London.

I grew up backstage, watching entertainers prepare for shows, learning every line, listening to the applause. It was there that I learned that it ***was*** possible to live outside the constraints of "normal" expectations. It was there that I first developed my own dreams and aspirations. And I am sure that set me on the road to overcoming the many obstructions that lay ahead.

Earlier, I talked about how we take our standards from the people around us. Some might be inspired by a teacher who helps them think bigger. Some might take their inspiration from someone they admire further afield. But very few would seriously expect that they themselves could become someone else's hero. I was lucky to have grown up in a family that was already outside the box. But **anyone can break the mold of normality if they believe in themselves, learn from the people who inspire them, and** (this is the most important part) **stick to their goals long enough to achieve them.**

At primary school, I had learned to do my own makeup for the school nativity play. (I was seven at the time, playing one of the three wise men.) As I grew, I was eager to learn other skills that might help me as a performer. I thought I would be a comedian, because they always had top billing. Whenever the teacher left the room, I would get up and tell jokes to the other kids. I wanted to be popular, but the other kids probably thought I was just weird. Fortunately, it's often the weird guys that later redefine the standards of normality.

As told you, when I was thirteen, my teacher had very negative opinions of what I would be capable of in the outside world. That was a shock for me. He assumed I would make no more effort than the other kids around me. At the age of eleven, I failed the exam that determined whether you were educated for an office job or relegated to be a manual worker, so it had been assumed that I wasn't going to be one of those "smart" people. I hadn't even realized it was a competition! That teacher's words hit home. They didn't have the effect he expected: to settle me down and prepare me to work in a factory. Instead, his words galvanized me to prove his opinion wrong. Ultimately, I thank my shortsighted teacher for that timely wake-up call.

I think that most of us drift through life with the people around us. We do what everyone does. We follow the life stages that society dictates. We are influenced by the expectations of our peers. My parents truly struggled to live an unconventional life, but they succeeded where others feared to try.

The biggest problem that we all face when trying to reach exceptional goals is the presumptions of the people around us.

My teacher presumed I was a dreamer, not a doer. He presumed I didn't have the talent or tenacity to make something special of my life. He presumed I would not pursue the people and situations that might eventually lead to success. He judged me by normal standards and presumed that I would fail. It is a tragedy that so many people let their lives be limited by other people's lack of imagination.

I admit that within the confines of those early years, my aspirations must have appeared ludicrous. My school was not renowned for producing high achievers. Even the head boy only qualified as proficient in three ordinary-level subjects. As untraditional as I might have seemed to those around me, nobody would ever have given credence to the idea that I would ever make a single movie or sell a single painting, let alone write this book.

My mother was the practical half of the family. She was a bookkeeper whose contribution helped keep the family afloat. An actor paired with a bookkeeper ... that made for a largely psychotic upbringing. But I credit my mum for the management skills that allowed me to develop into a businessman as well as an artist.

I starred in all the school plays that my teacher directed until, at fifteen, I objected to one production which I thought was stupid. I refused to be in it and unilaterally declared that I was going to produce my own play. And I did. To be honest, I was shocked

As a kid I thought my mum didn't love me. But now I look at these photos and can see that wasn't true

that nobody tried to stop me. But I directed the show and it was well-received. That was my first BIG step beyond what could have been expected of me.

Around that same time, my dad was teaching at drama school and one of his subjects was stage makeup. Three times a year, I earned pocket money during the weekend helping prepare the end-of-semester productions: nine shows, each with a cast of twenty performers, all of whom had to learn their makeup in a few hours. Dad would design what they needed and I helped them mix their colors effectively, shade their cheekbones, and sharpen their eyebrow pencils.

My mother was always amazed that I had the nerve to seize any opportunity that passed my way. I am sure that she thought I was getting above myself. But **the people who get noticed are often those who are bold to the brink of audacity**. In truth, on the inside, I was a scared kid afraid that if I didn't push the envelope, I might suffer the fate that teacher predicted.

So it was when I was seventeen that I answered the phone to someone who had called for my father. He was out. It was someone who wanted theatrical makeup artists for a job at the Royal Albert Hall (a very prestigious venue in the heart of London). They had no idea they were talking to a seventeen-year-old. I discussed

The low-income housing building where my dreams began

the job, made the booking, and negotiated a fee that was double what my dad would have asked. That was the first professional job that I did where, according to the event program, I was the boss and my dad was assisting me!

There is real value in the simplified vision of youth. Youngsters often achieve unlikely aims simply because they don't have enough experience to realize that they shouldn't be able to do what they just did. When you are older, you know all the pitfalls and that makes you wary and doubtful. But even when the going gets tough, **desperate situations have ways of sparking extreme creativity** and even projects that might seem impossible can be achieved.

When I was eighteen, I realized that people had been lying to me for years. I wasn't going to be tall and handsome! Raised in the theater, I knew that meant I wasn't going to have a significant career as a young performer. I didn't want to wait thirty years to be a character actor. So I looked at which skills I could offer that might still allow me to work in the entertainment industry.

It comes back to what I said about being the red tree in the forest. You need to look at what you have that others do not. Build on that. Makeup was my unusual skill, especially character makeup. So I used that foundation to get ahead.

I already had that job at the Royal Albert Hall to my credit. I figured that makeup people in theater are few and far between and poorly paid. Movies were more glamorous and much more lucrative, so I applied for a union card to work in movies. It was impossible to work in the movie studios without a union card. So with the optimism of youth, I sent in my application.

Of course, they ignored me.

I had a girlfriend at that time, Susan. Her very conservative parents hated me. Her father was managing director of a small department store. They saw me as a kid with zero prospects who was a problem to be overcome. Sometimes I was banned from the house. Later, they sent her to boarding school to get rid of me. So I struggled with uncertainty in my love life. I was living on hope on all levels.

Youngsters look at me now with my museum, my apartments, and my big reputation for doing BIG things and think, "What does he know about what I am going through?" But I know what it is to have nothing. (I thought the guy across the street was a big success because he had a ten-year-old car whilst I had to walk to school.) I know what it is to dream of a future that seems completely unattainable. I know what it is to have no physical resources to build a future with. (At that time there was no Internet to help me do it, either.) I sat in my tiny bedroom with a mix of helplessness and blind determination ... and I made a plan. I didn't know the specifics of how I would achieve that goal, but I made the plan anyway, writing poems to my girlfriend with an apparent confident maturity that I absolutely lacked.

During the course of my ill-fated relationship with Sue, at boarding school and beyond, there were long periods of separation and I corresponded in large part by letter. Her parents may have thought boarding school was a solution, but I remember traveling for two hours on Sunday mornings to sit on the wall outside her school and play my guitar (badly) as she and other young ladies filed out, two-by-two, on "church parade." I would meet her after church or slip her a note. It was very clandestine and definitely fit the romantic image I had of myself as the heroic vagabond.

During one of many periods when we were on the brink of breaking up, I sent her a letter that she must have thought was delusional. It was my plan, my vision for my future. I told her that her folks were wrong. I told her I ***could*** achieve the impossible. Extraordinarily, I wrote that I would become famous making movies. I said that I would write books and poetry and be well enough known to retire and become an artist at sixty. I explained that I would sell my paintings on the notoriety of my movie career and live an extraordinary life. (I couldn't paint to save my life at that time. But I had seen a movie with Kirk Douglas as Vincent Van Gogh and liked the idea of being an artist—as long as I didn't have to cut off my ear or die of an anti-social disease like Gauguin.)

*Days of Swamp and Servos* by Nick Maley

I have no idea how I could visualize, so accurately, the life I would ultimately come to live at a time when I had achieved virtually nothing. The letter didn't save the relationship. That fell apart over many years of long-distance interaction (and much anguish). But the visualization of the life I aimed to achieve became an important piece of the puzzle that drove me forward in the darkest moments of despair. It helped me shape the future I craved and the person that I wanted to be, despite years of negativity and the interminable obstacles life put in my way.

I guess I was about eighteen when my dad first got sick. My mother sheltered me from the details. It was mesothelioma. I took over his makeup classes at six drama schools across London. I thought it was a stopgap while he recovered. Instead, he spent several years slowly dying and I became a professional teacher at various drama institutions, including a college absorbed into Middlesex University. At first, I was nervous that they wouldn't like what I did and would let me go. (Insecurity plagues us all. The trick is not to let it show.) But they didn't fire me, and I taught there part-time for several years.

Now nineteen, I applied to get a movie union card again. I wrote explaining that I was nineteen years old and teaching at a university, claiming that I must be a whiz-kid. This time, I got an answer. It was one of those standard letters that said they had my info and would call if they needed me. Basically, don't call us, we'll call you. And at that point, any normal person would have given up and gone for plan B.

Instead, I researched where they held their union meetings and I showed up every month until they knew I wasn't going to go away, almost two years later. That was an extreme move. Radical thinking. But actually, a lot less effort than you might think.

There's a modern mindset that considers it smart to try to get by with as little effort as possible. But four hours a month for twenty-four months is less than three week's work. Not too much to ask in order to change the course of your life. And believe me, in the long run, those "smart" friends who make minimal effort will think ***you*** are the coolest for achieving your dreams while they live life to pay the bills.

So, it was in 1969 that I was invited to join the esteemed ranks of the makeup branch of NATTKE and enter the British film industry as a junior makeup artist. Those seven years of hard struggle had paid off, and I thought I had finally arrived as I worked alongside Charlton Heston, Richard Chamberlain, Sir John Gielgud, Christopher Lee, and more. However, I had only traversed the first hurdle. Soon I would face the realities of freelance living as I navigated long periods of unemployment. Those makeup chiefs who let me in already had old friends and trusted assistants that they would employ before me. I was in a new group with a new average. Now I had to find new ways to separate myself from the others to become the red tree in that specific forest.

I am not telling you all this to discourage you. I am trying to give you a practical insight on the long journey we all travel in order to live our dreams. Your goals may not be the same as mine, but the journey will still be fraught with diverse hurdles and obstacles. In reality, that is what keeps you sharp and focused. **You either buckle down and do whatever you must to reach your destiny, or you give up and spend fifty years wondering what might have been.**

It would be two more years before I worked with makeup maestro Stuart Freeborn and yet another five years before we made ***Star Wars***. (A full list of movies I contributed to follows this section.)

The first thing I did was subscribe to the industry periodicals. I read about who was doing what and where. I made notes of the heads of the makeup department, so I knew who worked the most and who got the best projects. I'm not good at sitting around, so making pretty people look prettier was going to wear thin. I wanted to make pretty people look pretty ugly. So I focused on the leading artists doing the best special makeup effects movies.

Of course there were still the naysayers who told me, "Don't bother with that effects stuff. The guys doing that have been doing it for twenty years. You'll never catch up." But the people who fail are the ones who give up—and that wasn't going to be me.

At the top of my list of leading makeup artists was Stuart Freeborn, who had a long career in character effects and also built the landmark apes for ***2001: A Space Odyssey***. Basically, I stalked him for two years. I sat near him at union meetings. I went to the studios where he was working and would sit at his table in the canteen at lunchtime. I made sure he knew who I was so that when his friends were not available, my name would stand out on the list.

In those difficult years, as I struggled to find work, tried to network with people that could help me, and endeavored to develop more employable skills, I kept thinking about that teacher who assumed that I would fail. Fear of having to tell him he was right kept me going another day, another week, another year.

I followed several basic principles to survive:

(i) I tried to get to work before the other guys and didn't leave until there was nothing left that I could help with. Even though I was not the most skilled person there, or the most charismatic, I was the most eager to help and learn. Ultimately, reliability is a valuable asset to any boss and he who makes the most effort (and doesn't screw up) is most likely to get the next job. **If you don't do your best, you are wasting the opportunity.**

(ii) Every morning, I looked at my list of questions and thoughts to see what I could do that day to get closer to my goal. This was key to edging closer to my dream. Never wait until tomorrow. **If you edge a little closer every day, eventually you *must* get there.**

(iii) I networked with everyone I could, even though some of those people didn't think much of me then, and I listened to the stories they told that held hidden tips that I might use another day. Unfortunately, my determination to make more effort than the others did not make me popular with some counterparts. They would tell me, "If you do that, they will expect us to do it, too." You can't please everyone. If they disliked me because they thought I was trying too hard, that's just another hurdle to overcome. There will also always be those cliquey people who hold you at a distance. Just remember that if you keep going, you will be the one left standing when the others drop by the wayside. I continued to make every effort on every job because I didn't know when I would get another opportunity.

(iv) Unfortunately, in the worst times of unemployment, I still needed to eat and pay rent. For a while, I continued with the security of freelance teaching. But as soon as I had to turn down a teaching appointment because I was doing a movie, the schools looked for someone else to fill my place. Even as you are moving up, there are losses as well as gains. I was hungry and facing the challenges we all meet at some point in our struggling career: I needed money from another source. Today, the Internet offers many opportunities for part-time income. That didn't exist at that time. I needed work in the morning that would leave me free in the afternoon when phone calls came for film work. And yes, I did some pretty menial jobs to get through until the next significant opportunity arose.

(v) When cash was really low, I filled my old car with gasoline so I could get to the next job. Then I walked everywhere or took the bus. I would show up at friends' houses at meal times and hope they took pity on me by sharing a little food. While my friends were finishing college and getting married, their new wives thought I was a flake and a dreamer. But they helped me with one edible handout after another. It was very tough. But I kept thinking of admitting I had failed, and that kept me going one day at a time. In so many ways this was the hardest time: I was on the fringe of achieving my goal, yet not getting enough opportunities to prove my worth or pay for luxury items. This is where so many people give up. It's also where networking is the most important and where your grit will be tested. **Tell yourself every day, "The people who fail are the ones who give up, and you have not failed until you give up."**

(vi) Between jobs, I could have played games or watched TV. Instead I strove daily to improve my skills by practicing where

I was weakest and adding new abilities that I thought might make me more competent. On each job, I tried to learn something from more experienced artists. While others sat around, I would volunteer for extra tasks that I thought might teach me something. I would reinvest a little of my earnings into equipment so I could practice those new skills at home. It was during this slow time of frequent unemployment that I acquired most of my basic professional skills, the tools that I put in "my toolbox" of capabilities. These skills made me able to nail additional tasks when the next opportunity arrived.

**Was I a fanatic? You bet. Because you don't succeed by being half-assed. Did people think I was crazy? Absolutely. But now they ask for my autograph.** Maybe now you understand why I say, **you can't live an exceptional life without making an exceptional effort.**

My efforts to stalk Stuart Freeborn finally paid off in 1971. He asked me to help on the movie ***Young Winston***, and I must have done okay because he employed me for two days and kept me on for sixteen weeks. We set off for location in Morocco, where we cavorted with belly dancers, argued with camels, and trudged across the Sahara Desert. I was sad as those four months came to a close, but I would help Stuart again periodically on other projects.

Another influence at this time was my friend and colleague Colin Arthur. Colin was considered by many to be a "loco" guy who worked all hours and prepared most of his jobs at home. Not in his garage or garden shed, either: Colin's whole house was a crazy creature shop. We prepared ***Sinbad and the Eye of the Tiger*** there, ***The Four Feathers***, and later, ***Clash of the Titans***.

Colin was always good at reducing costs and passing charges on to the production company. On ***The Four Feathers***, like other movies, he aimed to take his little convertible Triumph Herald on location where the company had to rent vehicles for the crew, and rent them his own car. As soon as we finished filming Jane Seymour at St. Pancras railway station at 5:00 PM one Friday, we jumped in the car and rushed to Colin's house in Putney. There we loaded everything needed for location in Spain and sped off to Dover, ninety-seven miles away, to catch the last ferry to France. We slept a little on the ship. Then he and I drove all night in relay and all the next day, until Saturday night we parked at the foot of the Pyrenees to rest.

I was never good at geography. It bored me with colored maps and statistics. But I loved this kind of crazy adventure as we experienced first-hand the changing cultures and landscape.

Six o'clock the next morning, we drove up the mountains to snow-covered Andorra, where Colin filled the car with bottles of booze. Then we rushed down the other side of the mountain range to the balmy hills and valleys of northern Spain.

Considering the race we were in to reach Almeria on the farthest southern coast, I was truly disturbed when Colin decided to take a four-hour detour to have supper in Barcelona. But it was Colin's car and Colin's job, so we went to Barcelona. It was around six PM that we reached the wide streets and majestic buildings of Spain's capital. He was taking us to a favorite restaurant of his on La Rambla, probably Barcelona's most famous boulevard where, Colin explained, young women walked in the afternoon, admired by their suitors and chaperoned by their grandmothers. What we encountered there was quite different.

In the central paved area milled a virtual army of policemen, armed with automatic weapons. Colin led the way through them as they grudgingly moved aside. We sat in the restaurant, considering the menu and wondering why the police were outside. What we didn't know was that Basque separatists were protesting farther down the street—but we soon found out as a riot ensued. The restauranteur rolled down his shutters as Colin ordered wine to the sound of machine guns and rubber bullets outside. I like adventure, but I have to admit I was more than a little nervous.

After dinner, we left and headed back to the car. Fortunately, our section of the street was deserted and there were no bodies on the ground. As we began to leave the city, we came to a metal barrier in the street, armed by a policeman. As Colin argued in Spanish that we ***must*** go down this road to get to our destination, I realized that it was the same street that we had just eaten in. The policeman, sick of arguing, opened the barrier and suddenly we were driving back into the boulevard. We didn't get far before we encountered a barricade of furniture built across the 100-meter-wide thoroughfare. Colin hopped out and immediately started moving the blockage. Protestors from the other end of the line came running and hurled furniture at us as the car sped through. Happy to have survived, I was stressed to see our way blocked by roadwork as Colin proposed that we turn around and run the blockade again. Fortunately, he listened to my protest and we found our way out through the backstreets.

That night we drove in relays again to arrive in Almeria by Monday morning, set up our location facilities, and start filming Tuesday. Crazy as it sounds, it was a life experience. One I will never forget.

I learned from Colin to never be off the clock, not to overwork things nobody will notice, and that sometimes quick and simple solutions can be as effective as things you labored over for weeks. I also learned not to argue with policemen.

Through the course of 1975-76, Graham Freeborn, Stuart's

son, asked me to help with some horror effects on commercials he was doing: Donald Pleasance, Frankenstein, Wolfman, and more all drinking lager in a bar. That led to him persuading his father, Stuart, to include me as the creature effects junior on a weird little Sci-Fi movie Stuart was preparing called ***The Star Wars***, later renamed ***Ep IV: A New Hope***.

At the time, it didn't seem like we were making history. I was just pleased to be working. Carrie, Mark, and Harrison were all unknown. It was a movie about gunslingers and wizards in space directed by a quiet guy who had made a movie about growing up in America in the fifties. How seriously could anyone take that?

**Stuart and Chewie on the set of *Star Wars Episode IV: A New Hope***

It was over a year before that job would bring us extraordinary credibility. The project changed my life. Our team built Chewbacca, Greedo, Bossk, and many more Mos Eisley creatures. When that project caught the public's imagination, we were suddenly flying as high as an X-wing.

You never know which project will hit big and which will flop. You have to give 120% to everything you do, because even those little projects may connect you to someone who opens the door to something big. Just as the horror ads led me to ***Star Wars***. I owe a ***lot*** to Graham, who became my closest friend in the business. Since his untimely passing, I have tried hard to share with fans the immense contribution he made to ***Star Wars*** and many other movies.

After ***A New Hope***, our team went on to ***Superman: The Movie*** and part of ***Superman II***. We did a pilot for Gene Roddenberry of ***Star Trek*** fame, then started on ***Episode V: The Empire Strikes Back***. I was over the hump in terms of getting work, but guess what? That was just the second hurdle. Now I was in a new group where the "norm" was much higher than before. I needed to work doubly hard to be the red tree in this new forest.

It was during this period that I met my wife-to-be, Gloria. She was an actress doing small parts in British TV dramas like ***Z Cars***, ***The Professionals***, and ***Doctor Who***. Fate brought us together

The makeup crew for *Episode V: The Empire Strikes Back* with some of the Yoda skins that I made. Photo © Lucasfilm Ltd

on a little horror movie. I pursued her for a while, and when she finally chose to put her faith in me, we formed a bond that has withstood the tests of the past forty-three years. I was blessed to find a partner who not only supported my career and shared many of my passions, but who also understood the focus and devotion it takes to follow your dreams. Of course, we didn't always agree. It takes a very special person to accompany a creative mind that doesn't apply standards that society considers normal, both privately as well as publicly. But she backed me through the twists and turns life threw at us and gave me the space I needed in order to be me. Nobody can ask more than that. When I excelled, she lifted me higher, and when I fell, she helped me back on my feet again. I couldn't have chosen a better life companion.

Having a wife added responsibility to the mix. It gave me a new perspective on life that reinforced my determination to succeed. I felt I had to show her (and the world) that she had been right to hitch her star to mine. The opportunity to do so came quite quickly, because now I was rubbing shoulders with industry leaders. I was seen as a rising member of England's premier creature effects team, and the ethic that had gotten me there continued to serve me well. I endeavored to learn anything I could from those techs from other departments, especially the expertise of Muppeteer Wendy Midener, who joined our team as Frank Oz's representative and contributed much to Yoda's development. I watched Stuart's progress closely as he advanced his personal variation of what would later become known as "animatronics," and I endeavored to convert tried-and-tested techniques into unusual formats that appeared to others to be new and innovative.

As a senior tech in the makeup workshop, I gained kudos building the Wampa with Graham, helped with the Tauntauns, designed, sculpted, and built the close-up Mynock, and created Dengar's scarred face. So when they needed a walking Yoda for long-distance shots and Stuart was busy, the line producer brought that job to me. I had made the Yoda molds with Stuart and foamed all the skins, so it wasn't too great a stretch to chemically enlarge a skin and create a mask to fit Deep Roy, one of the little people employed as a performer on the movie. The production team liked that and, as a result, asked me to work with special effects radio control supervisor Ron Hone and technician Dennis Lowe on a radio-controlled Yoda to go into Luke's backpack. They built the mechanism, I fitted the skins, completed fabrication, and helped Graham do the artwork. Finally, when the prototype animatronic puppet had some mechanical hiccups and the production was purportedly losing £70,000 a day waiting for repairs, Robert Watts and Bruce Sharman asked me if I could build a back-up puppet.

The walking Yoda animatronic (photo from OfficialPix.com, © Lucasfilm, LTD)

I could have stepped back and not taken the risk of falling on my face. But this was the opportunity of all opportunities. I believed I could do it. So, I gathered what courage I had, I simplified the principles that I had seen Stuart pursuing, and I built my first animatronic mechanism.

According to assistant Yoda puppeteer Dave Barclay, my back-up Yoda was used for 90% of Yoda's scenes. I was touched when associate producer Robert Watts later declared I had "fixed everything." That was the turning point in my career, and in my life. It was the culmination of all those years of effort, and it transformed the way people in the industry saw me. As I sat in the viewing theater behind George Lucas watching Yoda's "dailies," I knew we had done something nobody would forget, and there was a huge release of pressure that brought me close to tears. I didn't have to push myself so hard anymore (I thought), I didn't have to worry if there was money for food anymore. In that moment, I understood why my mother cried when she got her apartment. As fate would have it, it was the last full movie I would do with Stuart.

Because I had produced the back-up Yoda in such a short time, I had generated a notoriety for achieving jobs in record time. So when Director Lindsay Anderson needed to cut off Malcolm McDowell's head and have his naked, headless body strangle a nurse, spraying blood on a dozen members of the surgical staff, in his black comedy ***Britannia Hospital***, special effects supervisor George Gibbs asked me to step in to realize the effects. They needed 180 body parts ready to be sewn together, a full set of body prosthetics for Malcolm's Frankenstein-styled body make-up, his features on a removable head, a dummy body to spray blood, a separate animatronic body to sit up on the operating table, and prosthetic shoulders for a naked stunt man to stagger around in. We only had three weeks to prepare, and it was clear that this was ridiculously ambitious. But Gloria and I had bought our first house a few months earlier, and the bank manager was pushing for repayments. My ego didn't want to admit defeat and my principle of grasping every opportunity encouraged me to take on the "impossible" task. No words can convey how hard I worked for those three weeks with just an ex-flatmate and Colin Arthur's ex-girlfriend, Marion, to assist me. I don't think I went home more than twice a week. But I completed the task. Filming went well. The bank manager got paid, and my reputation for achieving the impossible was sealed.

Bruce Sharman, the production manager on ***The Empire Strikes Back***, had joined Jim Henson to produce ***Dark Crystal*** and ***Labyrinth***. He asked me to work on both films, but wanted to pay me less than before I worked on Yoda. Groundbreaking as they were, those were the first major movies I turned down.

Soon, people were asking me to be the head of department on new projects. First for smaller movies, and then on big movies, too. I was makeup supervisor on an adaptation of a Jackie Collins book and then nominated for an Emmy for my transformation of Anthony Hopkins into ***The Hunchback of Notre Dame***. Anthony Hopkins was a dream to work with: a kind and considerate man who treated me with such respect and humility. That rubbed off on me when, later, I was dealing with others who looked up to me as I looked up to Tony.

Turning Sir Anthony Hopkins into the Hunchback of Notre Dame

It was during this period that Gloria and I began the first of our non-movie adventures. What started as my keen interest in the zoological aspects of creature design and Gloria's acute love of animals quickly developed into a private zoo. We had miniature monkeys, BIG lizards, a collection of snakes, and a few parrots. Soon we were interfacing with London Zoo, who offered us some of their excess and older animals (it was hard to decline their offer of a puma cub). They even suggested we might write a paper on the breeding of Jackson's chameleons, which was one of our specialties. You see, we approached this new interest with the same dedication and devotion that I had applied for my movie work, and we achieved similar acclaim. **It is that persistence and determination which succeeds, whatever the application.**

Of course, some folks were not so happy about having us as their weird neighbors. Life has taught me that there are always those naysayers who want to put a spoke in your wheels. Someone called the RSPCA suggesting that we must be abusing animals. After the animal welfare people inspected us, they asked us to be an RSPCA safe-house and they gave us foxes, owls, kestrels, and more. That was a cherished stamp of approval.

We have many stories to tell about our animal days, more about the adventures that followed, and various humorous issues that touched our lives. Those deserve a book of their own. Many local kids came by to feed the animals and we hope that our attitude brushed off on some of them.

It was also during this time that we first visited the Caribbean, where we learned to scuba dive and drink piña coladas. Chilling under an umbrella with an azure sea lapping at my toes was an experience that stayed with me over the next few years.

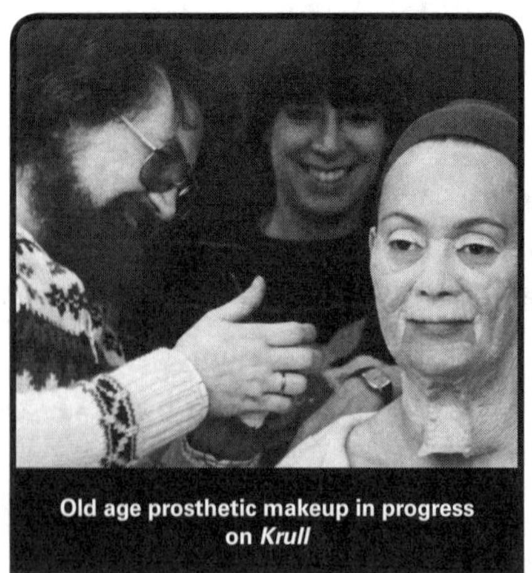
Old age prosthetic makeup in progress on *Krull*

By that time, my career as a designer of special makeup and creature effects was in full swing. I loved designing and building the creatures for ***Krull***, a forty-million-dollar project that was one of my biggest triumphs. Seeing my name in the big opening titles for the first time, rather than in the list at the end of the movie, was a thrill, too. The icing on the cake came when Marvel reproduced my work in comic books. My ego was very grateful. I was overjoyed when my idol, Dick Smith (who did ***The Exorcist***), described me as his "cherished colleague." He had mentored Rick Baker's early years and did the fantastic prosthetics for ***Little Big Man*** on Dustin Hoffman.

Shouldering the responsibility of being a head of department brought a new set of hurdles. That didn't truly come home to me until I joined the team creating Michael Mann's ***The Keep***. On ***Krull***, the production team gave me space to create the prosthetic and creature effects pretty much as I chose to create them. They appreciated that I was short on time and gave me the latitude to get the job done on schedule. It seems extraordinary that the next job I did was the complete opposite. It was like leaving the Jedi and joining the Sith.

Michael was the writer, the director, and a producer of ***The Keep***. He had a series of concepts in his head that might have been fantastic. But nothing anyone did seemed to live up to his vision. Sometimes, it appeared that his vision varied on a daily basis. We lost a lot of time doing hundreds of tests. He had me build animatronic figures when I had advised that we would get better results from a creature suit, then had me rebuild the creature as a creature suit. I was working insane hours again—over ninety hours every week. At one point, I hadn't been home for two nights. On the third night, I finished what I needed for the next day at 3:00 AM and decided to drive home for a shower. I stopped at a red light and fell asleep while waiting for it to turn green. It was 5:40 AM when I awoke, still sitting at the traffic lights. It was too late to get home. I turned around and went back to the studio.

Halfway through production, we became aware that Michael was rewriting the script each night. Revisions are not uncommon on many productions, but in this case, he was rewriting scenes for the next day's filming. So people came to work prepared for sequences that were scrapped, and nobody knew what they were filming that day. In consequence of this apparent chaos, the production overran by nine months. There were eight nervous breakdowns, and I was on the brink of being the ninth by the time I left the movie. Ultimately, I was disappointed in Michael, and he was disappointed in me. For the first time, I began to question whether being head of department was something I wanted to do for the rest of my life.

Gloria and I returned to the Caribbean, this time for a month. We went diving every day. It was the most relaxing experience I could imagine, playing with fish and turtles and being one with nature. Gloria and my love affair with the islands really began then, and the seed of relocation was sown.

I returned to do a movie in Hungary with George Clooney, Charlie Sheen, and Laura Dern, who were virtually unknown at that time. Then I moved on to the biggest technical challenge of my career, ***Lifeforce***, an everyday story of soul-sucking vampires from outer space.

Up until that time, my biggest crew had consisted of about twenty FX artists. But ***Lifeforce*** was a cascade of creature effects every few minutes, with extraordinary live-action transformation sequences. As a result, I needed a team of almost seventy varied talents to assist me. As always, preproduction time was short, just six weeks. Director Tobe Hooper graciously allowed me to do what I thought best. Along the way, I rewrote some sequences and worked with writer Dan O'Bannon to invent others. I had my own unit to film the animatronic sequences I devised, and I really felt that I was at the cutting-edge of creature effects again.

I was touched when one day Jim Henson came to my set as I filmed the demise of a vampire bat alien on the steps of St. Paul's Cathedral. He personally asked me to go work with him on ***Return to Oz***. But sadly, our schedules and personnel preferences did not mesh.

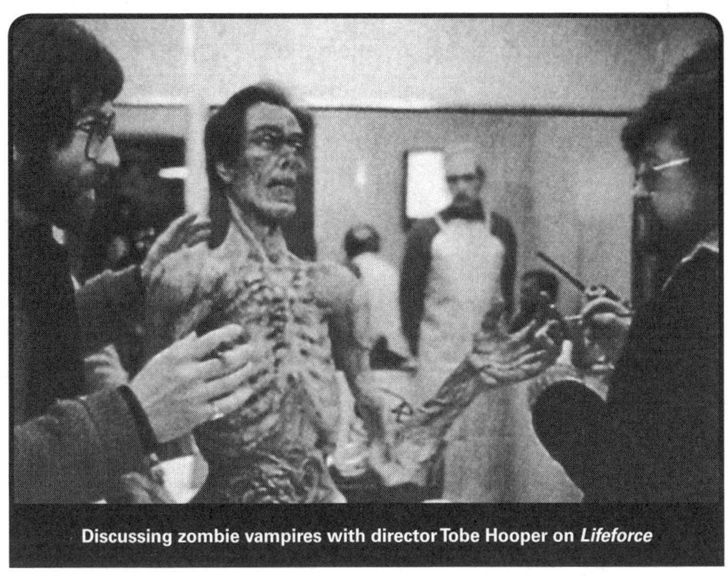

**Discussing zombie vampires with director Tobe Hooper on *Lifeforce***

Today, I take great pride in the number of talented youngsters whose careers either started or were uplifted with me—more on ***Lifeforce*** than any other. Bob Keen, who was my close aid for many years, designed creature effects for the ***Hellraiser*** movies. Jean Bolte, who started by doing wigs for my department on ***Lifeforce***, carved a big reputation as a visual effects artist at Industrial Light and Magic. Daniel Parker did his first prosthetics makeups with me also, and later became a leader in his field with awards for best makeup on ***Cloud Atlas*** and ***Mary Shelley's Frankenstein***. My former housemate, Denise Horsham (Kelly), did two movies with me before administrating a major camera rental company in Pinewood Studios and becoming manager of post-production for United International Pictures, working on projects for Paramount Pictures and DreamWorks. David White, who started with me at sixteen, was recently honored by being inducted into the Academy of Motion Pictures Arts USA and won multiple awards and nominations for his work on ***Guardians of the Galaxy***, ***La Vie en Rose***, ***Captain America***, and ***Maleficent***. Jill Hooper, who had helped Gloria with the animals part-time for two years before coming to work for me at the movie studio when she was eighteen, had an outstanding movie career that culminated in her becoming a producer for Steven Spielberg's DreamWorks. Stephen Norrington was sixteen years old when he joined my crew on ***Lifeforce***. He went on to reprise the chestburster for ***Aliens*** and direct ***Blade*** and ***League of Extraordinary Gentleman***. Today, I try to continue that tradition of "encouragement by example" through my foundation and have had several successes there, too.

As my FX sequences on ***Lifeforce*** were being completed, Tobe kept telling me, "You'll get an Oscar for this!" But unfortunately, this horror, vampire, zombie movie with sexual overtones was too far ahead of its time. A movie that is not well received by the critics doesn't get nominated for the industry's highest awards. It was undoubtedly my best work; it won a Saturn Award and today is considered a cult classic.

I don't want this section to evolve into a series of tales about the movies that I made. This book is not meant to be about that. It's about the rewards that come from persistence and the mindset needed to break through the barriers fate puts before you. It's about discovering that your preconceptions are less rewarding than you imagined and having the courage to set a course for new horizons. In this section, I just want to demonstrate the changing panorama of life's challenges and how I used the principles that I outline in this book to face uncertainty in order to walk a path that others only dream about. If tales about the movies that I made appeal to you, the last section of this book gives a brief insight into many classics and others long forgotten. Here, let me move on to the events that led me to take my life in a new direction.

A ten-day stint on Duran Duran's Grammy-winning music video ***Wild Boys*** forged an outstanding working relationship with director Russel Mulcahy. I was thrilled when he later invited me to join him in preproduction for the first ***Highlander*** movie. The script was inspiring and original. I could immediately see the potential for a big hit as I devised the storyboards for all the "Quickening" sequences, prepared prosthetics for the Kurgan, anticipated how to make each beheading different and anticipated, once again, to direct my own FX unit. But as much as this was my dream come true, I hadn't foreseen the politics, egos, and personalities that were about to engulf me. A series of production decisions added four hours to my already-over-extended days. I became exhausted with an ever-expanding workload. The last straw came when the cinematographer, a very old-school guy, learned that I—with only a makeup union card—was rewriting sequences, developing storyboards, and was scheduled to direct second unit. He couldn't accept that and began undermining everything I was doing. At that point, my load became unbearable and exhaustion overwhelmed me.

As I anticipated, the movie was great, but it was a nightmare to make and, in its wake, I was left questioning the direction my life was taken. It wasn't just about developing special makeup and creature effects anymore. It was about politics, admin, budgets and schedules, housing equipment, finding new talent, developing ***their*** skills and keeping ***them*** employed. None of these things had anything to do with the artistic creativity that had driven me to make movies initially. I had adapted to these new challenges and built a significant reputation, but I wasn't happy on 65% of productions and was truly miserable on 20%. Having contributed to over sixty movie and music projects, my enthusiasm for working in the film industry was seriously tarnished. It wasn't that I tired of the creativity. I loved that. But I was being worn down by producers and directors who would employ an expert, but not listen to his practical advice. I was tired of the meetings and the interdepartmental politics.

I have been quick to tell others that if they don't have a passion for what they are doing, it's time to do something else. It is hard to walk away from something that provides a good income. But what is the value of a big house and fast cars if they don't bring you lasting satisfaction? So, unexpectedly, one day I told Gloria that I wanted to explore new horizons. Bless her heart, she would follow me anywhere. And she did.

Some might think that the journey that had led me to this point was somewhat pointless if I then turned away to explore pastures new. But that is far from the truth. My journey was a series of great experiences that prepared me for the adventures yet to come. **Over time, you will learn that it's the journey that makes life interesting, rarely the destination.** The horizons you reach are not always the places you thought they would be. But every time you reach that distant goal, you discover new horizons from the perspective of your new vantage point. New horizons generate new goals, and with them come new challenges.

So, we set off in search of a sailing yacht. Not that we knew how to sail. Buying a boat was the solution to a problem. It was a cheap means of transport and a place to live, rent free, wherever we arrived. It made the possibility of a year in the Caribbean a practical expectation. I read two books on sailing theory. We bought a forty-foot Jeanneau Sunfiz and set off to test our skills against the ocean. What a fantastic life experience that turned out to be as we dodged hurricanes, snorkeled for supper, sailed by moonlight, or watched the sun go down from the cockpit of our little boat.

Every stage of life presents something new to be overcome. If your challenges are always the same, you're not progressing. If you don't progress, you can't reach new heights. Safe is comfortable, but it is also boring. Fresh challenges keep your brain sharp and ultimately keep you young.

We could never find a good excuse to abandon the Caribbean and return full time to our old lifestyle. After nine months afloat, we rented a little BWIA house where I started painting to express some of the things I had witnessed on our voyages. Soon after, someone suggested I show my paintings at a prestigious hotel where tourists might buy them. They say that you can't make a living as an artist but actually, it was very easy, and soon I had a Caribbean art gallery that was recommended shopping on all the major cruise lines.

Of course, I didn't abandon entertainment entirely. I made videos for the government of Antigua; designed stages for fashion shows, Carnival, and Miss World; directed music videos in Holly-

**Nick (front center) representing Antigua in cruising class at Antigua Sailing Week 1999**

wood; and consulted on creature effects in Germany. Each episode and endeavor—becoming president of the Antigua Art Society, co-ordinating exhibitions in museums, becoming commodore of a local yacht club, representing island nations in big regattas, traveling the world as a guest speaker at movie conventions and comic cons, and even founding my little non-profit museum and writing this book with the hope of encouraging ***you*** to follow ***your*** dreams—each project encompassed new goals, presented unique problems, and fresh triumphs. Each was conquered using the same attitude and the same set of principles that brought me success in movies, as outlined in previous passages.

I told you that one of the movies I contributed to was ***Superman***. I hope this brief glimpse at the hills and valleys of my life will demonstrate that a starry-eyed kid from low-income housing can fly, too. If a dreamer like me can soar to unlikely heights, rubbing shoulders with some of the biggest stars, grasping improbable opportunities, and dealing with whatever challenges lay in his way, then so can you.

Thanks for reading. Have a ***great*** life!

If you like the ideas in my little book of BIG ideas enough to share them with friends, family, or associates, take care to follow your own advice and please leave a review at "The Do or Do Not Outlook" on Facebook.

# MOVIES & ENTERTAINMENT

## FILMOGRAPHY & NOTES

I began making movies in 1969, one of only ten makeup artists granted a union card to work in the British film industry since 1954. A few of the other artists in that group fell by the wayside over the years. Others achieved recognition quickly with landmark movies. My road to acclaim was long and meandering. Here are a few memories from that journey.

These movies are listed by their release date, but we were making them a year or so before.

### ■ 1970 – *Julius Caesar* – Commonwealth United Entertainment

A curious adaptation of William Shakespeare's play starring Charlton Heston as Mark Anthony. It was littered with big names. You would think it must have been exciting, rubbing shoulders with the likes of Richard Chamberlain (***Dr. Kildare***), Christopher Lee (Dracula and later Count Dooku in ***Star Wars***), Robert Vaughn (***The Man from U.N.C.L.E***), Diana Rigg (***The Avengers***), and many other stars. But I was the new kid on the block—the most junior "assistant makeup artist"—and I was tasked to help with 400 lily-white English background extras who were playing the plebeian populous of Rome. My days were fraught with endless rounds of body makeup, fake tan after fake tan, and the more experienced makeup guys happily gave me the very worst of jobs. "You can do the legs and feet," I was told. And as the new guy, I buckled down daily with a breaking back to 800 legs and too many bouts of athlete's foot. This wasn't what I had worked so hard to attain, but I wasn't going to be put off by their unkind prank. When you are the junior, you grin and bear it.

After just three weeks, I was plunged into the harsh reality of freelance work during several months of unemployment while I waited for another break.

### ■ 1971 — *The Music Lovers* — United Artists / Russ Films

The first Ken Russell movie I assisted on. Russell's movies were always prestigious but always highly sexual. This was no exception. It starred Richard Chamberlain and Glenda Jackson and revolved around Tchaikovsky's struggle with his sexual preferences. It was on this movie that I saw in detail how other makeup artists dressed false beards in preparation for the next day's shoot. Many avoided this "chore." I volunteered in order to get more experience and, fortunately, my less-seasoned efforts were not frowned upon. Nineteen seventy-one was a very slow year for me, but I acquired a false beard and a book on period styles and spent many hours dressing and redressing that beard in different ways until I became quite expert at it.

As bills mounted and options dwindled, I spent a few months as a business machines salesman. I was better at dressing beards.

### ■ 1972 – *Young Winston* – Columbia Pictures Corporation – directed by Sir Richard Attenborough

Stuart Freeborn was a makeup and creature designer I longed to work with. He had four decades of outstanding work, from ***Oliver Twist*** in 1948 to three characters on Peter Sellers for ***Dr. Strangelove***, and the groundbreaking apes in Kubrick's ***2001: A Space Odyssey***. I had stalked him on and off for many months. So my heart raced when Stuart offered me two day's work on this historical film with stars like Robert Shaw, Anne Bancroft, Jack Hawkins, Ian Holm, Anthony Hopkins, and John Mills. It was only my third significant film, but I wanted to impress Stuart with my character work. I was in luck. We were recreating two hundred members of the British parliament set in the 1890's, which gave me the chance to display my newly acquired beard skills.

My two days led to several weeks and an invitation to join Stuart on location in the sweltering sands of Morocco. Imagine me stepping out of a council flat (low-income housing) when a Rolls Royce arrived to take me to the airport for my first film location. Daily we turned Moroccans into English cavalrymen and Whirling Dervishes. The most important consequence of this movie was befriending Stuart's son, Graham Freeborn. A very talented yet little-known artist that I tell more about later. He became a lifelong associate.

### ■ 1972 — *Alice's Adventures in Wonderland* — Fox-Rank Distributors

I had thought this would be my chance to delve into creature effects as Stuart (Freeborn) assembled a team to turn Peter Sellers into the March Hare, Dudley Moore into the Dormouse, Michael Crawford into the White Rabbit, Spike Milligan into the Gryphon, Sir Ralph Richardson into the Caterpillar, Dame Flora Robson into the Queen of Hearts, and so many more. But Stuart didn't use me for any of those juicy jobs and after a few weeks of straight make-ups, I was unemployed again.

It was great to see what mastery could be achieved; yet frustrating to be so close, and yet so far away.

### ■ 1973 — *The Glass Menagerie* — ABC TV - with Katharine Hepburn and Sam Waterston

Having struggled with another bout of unemployment, finding myself talking to legendary Hollywood star Katharine Hepburn and experiencing her caring and down-to-earth attitude had a great impact on me. She took time to talk to the little people like me with encouraging words and a kind heart. It came at a time when my spirits needed lifting, and that principle of encouragement has stayed with me over the years. The rumor was that young Sam Waterston was destined to be the new Marlon Brando. That didn't exactly work out for him, and it was decades before I saw him again in the TV series ***Law & Order***.

**■ 1973 — *The Nelson Affair* aka *Bequest to the Nation* - Universal Pictures (aka MCA/Universal Pictures) — with Glenda Jackson, Peter Finch, and Anthony Quayle**

The second Glenda Jackson movie where I assisted Wally Schneiderman, another veteran British chief makeup artist. It was an uninspiring job, listening to the old makeup men talking about working with Greta Garbo and Betty Davis. They seemed bitter that, in their latter years, they were back to doing menial jobs with the crowd. I told myself that when my passion died as theirs had, I would move on to new horizons.

**■ 1974 — *Undercovers Hero* aka *Soft Beds and Hard Battles* — Charter Film Productions and the Rank Organization — with Peter Sellers**

My third movie with Stuart Freeborn. A wild World War II comedy where Peter Sellers played multiple parts. Peter had the crew in fits of laughter as he romped with some very sensuous young actresses. Liza Minnelli came to the set to visit him. They were engaged ... for a month!

### ■ 1974 — *Figaro* — Anvil Productions

Anvil was a very small company specializing in educational films and shorts. This film version of the famed opera was only a two-week production, but my first as makeup supervisor. It led to another short film where I made Sir Ralph Richardson into the Ghost of King John. It was my first fantasy effects makeup on a prestigious leading actor. Sir Ralph was a legend of the silver screen, having been knighted in the 1940's. I was careful to treat him with the respect he deserved. But he gave me the greatest encouragement when he complimented me on my work and encouraged me to continue with my craft; a very charming man.

### ■ 1974 — *The Man with the Golden Gun* — United Artists — with Roger Moore, Christopher Lee, and Britt Ekland

This was a movie where the makeup was supervised by my colleague, Paul Engelen. He and I had gotten our union ticket on the same day and we were similar ages. I was in awe that Paul was already chiefing major motion pictures. But life seemed to have blessed Paul. He was a handsome, charismatic young man with a spectacular smile and an E-type Jaguar. Extraordinarily, he was a nice guy, too! Years later, he would be instrumental in creating another classic ***Star Wars*** character: Darth Maul.

In honesty, my only claim to ***The Man with the Golden Gun*** was spending four days doing the glamour and full-body makeups on the naked girls in the title sequence. It was tougher than you might imagine.

■ **1975 — *That Lucky Touch* — Gloria Films — with Roger Moore, Susannah York, Shelley Winters, and Lee J. Cobb**

Another short job assisting Paul.

■ **1975 — *Legend of the Werewolf* — Tyburn Film Productions Limited — with Peter Cushing, Ron Moody, and Hugh Griffith**

Graham Freeborn had become my closest friend in the industry. He was responsible for makeup and creature effects on this variation on the werewolf story. I had moved to a bedsit in Teddington where he lived and helped him with other FX jobs around this time. I remember particularly some horror-based beer commercials with Donald Pleasance. This was my testing ground for FX makeup and when Graham was asked to do this job, I assisted him.

■ **1976 — *Shout at the Devil* — Hemdale/AIP**

The third Roger Moore movie where I assisted my friend, Paul Engelen. The movie filmed in Malta with Lee Marvin, Ian Holm, and the delectable Barbara Parkins. Part of Barbara's appeal in real life was that she was tiny, like a sparrow, her hand so fragile,

as we were introduced. Yet her on-screen presence was always formidable.

Lee was formidable, too, with a big reputation as a heavy drinker. I remember one Sunday in the hotel, watching publicity on TV about how Lee Marvin was on the wagon. That same day, he fell into the hotel pool blind drunk. What a character.

**■ 1976 – *The Incredible Sarah* – Cinema International Corp**

Another job starring Glenda Jackson as Sarah Bernhardt. Once again, I assisted Wally Schneiderman. More beard work.

**■ 1976 – *Evil Heritage* aka *Satan's Slave* – Monumental Films**

My second movie as makeup supervisor. This tiny, independent movie was made on a shoestring by a handful of movie technicians. The budget was so low that, in one scene, other crew members and I donned robes to become "mad monks" that chased the heroine through the countryside. But this movie had a lasting impact upon my life. It was then that I met my wife-to-be, the beautiful Gloria Walker. Gloria had a small part in the movie which required prosthetic effects done by a colleague, Robin Grantham. We were shooting late one night when Robin covered Gloria in prosthetics and fake blood. As we were shooting later and later, he asked me to take care of her while he went to an end-of-production party for

*The Incredible Sarah*. The day's filming came to a wrap and I removed the prosthetics from her blood-stained hair and body, then waited outside the bathroom door while she took a bath to remove the residue. I was pretty sure that the stains would not come off. Thirty minutes later, I was scrubbing her down in the bath and we got quite well-acquainted. We didn't date straight away. But three years later we were married and, at the wedding reception, the producers of the movie said, "Don't blame us." Forty-three years later we are still hanging out together.

### ■ 1976 — *The Boys are Back in Town* — Thin Lizzy album cover

This was my first venture into the music world. I was asked to make the band look like they had been in a big fight and covered them in scratches, cuts, and bruises. I guess I did the job too well because, ultimately, the work was considered too gruesome to be used.

### ■ 1977 — *Sinbad and the Eye of the Tiger* — Columbia Pictures — with Patrick Wayne and Jane Seymour

I was helping my friend, makeup effects designer Colin Arthur, who was creating live-action characters for inserts that needed to match the stop-motion sequences filmed by the legendary Ray Harryhausen. I did a little pre-production on the golden Minotaur suit. Inside that suit, making his first film, was a hospital porter named Peter Mayhew. Peter was the second-tallest man in England at seven feet, two inches tall. He was so good natured in that and another, more difficult creature suit that later that year, the production supervisor and I recommended Peter to play a key role in another notable film: Chewbacca in ***Star Wars***.

### ■ 1977 – *One of the Boys* (Music Video) – with Roger Daltry from The Who

A fun job where I made Roger into several characters including a punk and a teddy boy. In those days, the top tax bracket in England was 96%. When I heard Roger came to work one day by helicopter, I commented that was somewhat excessive, Roger responded, "I don't own that helicopter; 96% is owned by the government!"

### ■ 1977 – *Star Wars IV: A New Hope* – 20th Century Fox / Lucasfilm Ltd – directed by George Lucas – with Harrison Ford, Mark Hamill, Carrie Fisher, Peter Cushing, and Sir Alec Guinness

Helping my friend, Graham Freeborn, with several small prosthetics projects finally brought its reward when Graham persuaded Stuart to include me on the creature FX team for the Mos Eisley cantina sequence. I helped build Greedo, Snaggletooth, and made eyes for most of the characters that Graham had sculpted for principal photography. I assisted Stuart with a third hand when he needed it for Chewbacca, too. A great step forward for me was to work with Graham specializing in the foam latex process, which was largely a secret in those days. I sculpted hands for Pondo, whose arm was cut off, and at last was an integral part of Britain's premier makeup effects team.

We had only eight weeks to fill that bar with aliens and film the master shots. Later, in post-production, George Lucas would raise extra money to add inserts. Extra creatures were created in the USA, based on some great illustrations by Ron Cobb. They included the cantina's famed band and other popular wretches in that hive of scum and villainy.

**Nick and other members of the creature crew on Star Wars Episode IV: A New Hope**

People ask what the stars were like back then. They were all unknown at that time. Mark was, and is, a very nice guy. Very funny. He kept us entertained. Carrie was ... well, Carrie, a Hollywood princess with habits to match. Harrison was the quieter one, often reading a book. None of us who worked on that project could ever have guessed that this under-budget sci-fi movie, with gunslingers and wizards in space, would change the way movies were made forever.

■ **1977 — *Spectre* - 20th Century Fox TV / A Gene Roddenberry Production — with John Hurt, Robert Culp, and Gig Young**

Today, people might think that working for ***Star Trek*** creator Gene Roddenberry was somewhat treacherous for a ***Star Wars*** alumni. But ***Star Wars*** had not yet been released, and ***Star Trek*** was actually a much bigger name at that time. Unfortunately, this "inner-space" story with demons and black magic was not well-written and never achieved ***Star Trek*** status.

■ **1977 — *Disraeli: Portrait of a Romantic* — Thames TV — with Ian McShane**

Another job where I made prosthetic appliances for my friend, Colin Arthur.

### 1977 — *A Bridge Too Far* — United Artists

My second movie with director Sir Richard Attenborough starring a huge array of big names including Robert Redford, Dirk Bogarde, Sean Connery, Ryan O'Neal, Gene Hackman, Michael Caine, Anthony Hopkins, James Caan, Maximilian Schell, Elliott Gould, and Sir Laurence Olivier. I spent five months in Holland assisting makeup supervisor Tom Smith and specializing in creating up to 400 wounded soldiers daily. It was an Oscar-winning epic about the tragic events of the battle of Arnhem in World War II.

*A Bridge Too Far*

### ■ 1977 — *Valentino* — United Artists

Another sexy Ken Russell movie, this time starring ballet dancer Rudolf Nureyev. We took over the ballroom at Blackpool Tower to film a boxing sequence with 500 local women as extras in the audience. Of all the crew members dealing with the crowd, only two of us were not gay. It was a memorable experience.

### ■ 1978 — *Superman: The Movie* — Warner Bros

Yet another star-studded production with Marlon Brando, Gene Hackman, Christopher Reeve, Glenn Ford, Margot Kidder, and Susannah York. I was assisting Stuart Freeborn again; we created 160 dummies for different sequences. Often people ask me, "What makeup effects were there in ***Superman***?" But Chris Reeves couldn't fly. We made numerous models, from twelve-inch versions to full-sized figures. We made a miniature Lois Lane to fly over the city and all the super villains to float through space. There were also life-sized dummies of Marlon Brando and Gene Hackman for varied shots, cats to be rescued from trees (you can't staple a cat to a tree and swing a guy on wires to pick it up), polar bears to swim toward the ice fortress, and little boys to go over Niagara Falls. All were physical effects. Chris was a really nice guy. Dave Prowse, who played Darth Vader, was employed to help Chris add muscle mass. But in case he failed to bulk up enough, we made a set of prosthetic muscles for him, too. Chris put on enough muscle not to need the suit, so Graham and I wore the muscles to the bar instead.

**■ 1978 — *The Parkerilla* (Album Cover) — Graham Parker**

A half-human, half-gorilla makeup for this British rocker.

**■ 1978 — *The Four Feathers* — Rosemont Productions**

A TV remake of this classic tale with Beau Bridges, Jane Seymour, Richard Johnson, and Robert Powell. Another job assisting Colin Arthur. We drove from London to the southern tip of Spain to film the location sequences. I would soon evolve into a married man and I am grateful to Colin, who helped to keep me employed during this period of uncertainty. I was doing makeup on Robert Powell, a big star at that time having done a remarkable job playing Jesus of Nazareth in the NBC TV series of the same name.

Producer Norman Rosemont was renowned for being very tight on expenditure. One of the stars responded by having a T-shirt printed saying, "***The Four Feathers***: A Roman Nosemont Production."

**■ 1978 — *The Thief of Baghdad* — Studios de la Victorine**

Another remake, with Roddy McDowall and Peter Ustinov. This

time I was assisting another colleague who would soon be assisting me on bigger productions. It was interesting to watch a remotely controlled rig for the flying carpet that actually carried actors high above the ground. But I was mostly impressed to work with Peter Ustinov, who kept us amused with tales of his exploits on other movies.

### ■ 1978 — *Absolution* — Universal Pictures

A psychological thriller with Richard Burton and Billy Connolly. I was brought onto this movie in post-production to create a close-up effects head of a young man to be stoved in with a shovel by Richard Burton. I made a pressurized skull with reservoirs filled with blood and set that inside gelatin flesh with a plastic skin. No matter where it was hit, it would bleed. They filmed it in slow motion and the "clapper/loader," the youngest of the camera crew, went to the bathroom to throw up. Once again, my work was so effectively gruesome that the director eventually chose to use just a quick-cut in the final edit.

### ■ 1979 — *Bloodline* — Geria III-Produktion München

This German-based production of a Sidney Sheldon book passed through London as part of its location sequences, and I helped the German makeup supervisor as he worked with Audrey Hepburn,

James Mason, and Omar Sharif. I was very impressed by the humility of both Audrey Hepburn and James Mason (I didn't interact with Omar), who were massive stars when I was growing up.

■ **1979 — *The World is Full of Married Men* — New Line Cinema**

From a book by Jackie Collins. I was employed as makeup supervisor with Anthony Franciosa, Carroll Baker, and Anthony Steel. This was largely a traumatic movie for me, where I balanced my desire to make a good impression with the reality of dealing with a major performer who had a debilitating drug habit. In contrast, Carroll Baker, very much in control of her career, gave me instructions on how she expected me to recreate her classic look, designed for her in Hollywood seventeen years before, for Kubrick's ***Lolita***. I had hoped to update that for her, but she wanted none of that. Later, when she saw the glamour makeup that I did on newcomer Sherrie Lee Cronn, she grudgingly told me, "You have quite a bit of talent." I was happy to accept the compliment.

■ **1980 — *The Shining* — Warner Bros. / Hawk Films — directed by Stanley Kubrick**

With Jack Nicholson and Shelley Duvall, this movie quickly became a classic. I came onboard to help makeup supervisor Tom Smith with the ghosts in the ballroom and the maggot-riddled old lady in the bath. Kubrick wanted to test everything in a tedious manner. Jack Nicholson was not easy, either; it seemed like he was "in character" all the time.

■ **1980 — *Superman II* — Warner Bros**

Although this came out in 1980, we actually filmed half this movie at the same time as ***Superman: The Movie***.

■ **1980 — *Flash Gordon* — Dino De Laurentiis Company**

This largely Italian production starred Max von Sydow, Sam J. Jones, Topol, Timothy Dalton, Robbie Coltrane, and many more. There were many ego conflicts between the Italian and English crews, and I was brought in as a prosthetics consultant making super long fingernails for Ming and his daughter.

■ **1980 — *Three on the Run* — Animatronics Ltd**

This pilot for a children's comedic TV series included a fully animatronic bear suit and starred Louis Gossett Jr. It was the first time that I directed the special makeup effects unit, which actually amounted to pretty much the entire pilot.

### ■ 1980 — *The Awakening* — Orion Pictures / Warner Bros

This was another movie where I was brought on in post-production. They wanted a sequence where actress Stephanie Zimbalist's face showed signs of being chiseled away, similar to an Egyptian mummy earlier in the film and another sequence where she looked like the same mummy until she smiled and her face cracked. Stephanie was very cooperative, and shooting was very successful. Charlton Heston was the big name in the movie. He was now in his late sixties and not as macho as he had been in my first movie eleven years earlier. Not many people know that he had three toupees. The hair on each was a little longer than the previous. Every week, he would change to one a little longer. Then, after three weeks, he went back to the first as if he had been for a haircut. He didn't share this with anyone; not even the production hairdresser, who was afraid to tell him that his toupees needed attention. She resorted to asking me to pat down extruding hairs when I went in to take the shine off his nose.

### ■ 1980 — *Star Wars V: The Empire Strikes Back* — Chapter II Productions / 20th Century Fox/ Lucasfilm Ltd

This movie was my thirty-fifth professional project, but it was the turning point in my career. I contributed to the Wampa, the Tauntaun, the Ugnaughts; designed, sculpted, and built the

Mynock head; and worked on all four versions of Yoda. This was the movie where I got noticed as a key contributor to what is generally accepted as the most popular of the classic ***Star Wars*** trilogy, and it opened doors for me over the next few years. I assembled three versions of Yoda, most notably, I built the back-up Yoda seen in 90% of Yoda's sequences. The back-up was constructed in sixty hours over three days from the skins and skulls we had around the workshop. This fueled my reputation of pulling a miracle out of the hat at short notice—a reputation that would follow me for many years.

***Star Wars V: The Empire Strikes Back***

**■ 1980 – *The Mouse and the Woman* – Alvicar / Facelift Films Ltd**

Whilst making ***The Empire Strikes Back***, I was traveling to Wales on Saturday night to film the prosthetics for this movie on Sunday, then driving back again. It was a very small independent production.

**■ 1981 – *Clash of the Titans* – Metro-Goldwyn-Mayer**

I made prosthetics for Colin Arthur's masks on this classic film with Burgess Meredith, Sir Laurence Olivier, Ursula Andress, Claire Bloom, Dame Maggie Smith, and Dame Flora Robson.

**■ 1981 – *Inseminoid* aka *Horror Planet* – Jupiter Film Productions**

At this time, I had a small workshop in Shepperton Studios. One day, on my way to the canteen, I met Norman Warren, who had directed ***Evil Heritage***. He seemed downcast and explained that he had been preparing a small independent movie, but differences with the writer had resulted in the script being withdrawn. He had the money, but no movie. I asked him what he was looking for and he told me sci-fi horror. I went home and in four days Gloria and I wrote ***Inseminoid***. Three days later, we sold it to Jupiter Films. I designed and built the prosthetic and creature effects for the movie and was pleased when the budget was doubled and the cast included Judy Geeson, Victoria Tennant, and Stephanie Beacham. It included my second on-screen performance when I puppeteered the alien babies I created. Ultimately, this became a very eye-opening and disappointing experience. The script we wrote was about an alien scientist, the last of his species, unwittingly released from suspended animation by a team of astro-archeologists examining the ruins of their other-worldly civilization. To procreate his species and save it from extinction, he inseminates a female crew member who goes crazy to feed her rapidly growing embryos. This causes devastation amongst the archeological crew. But the movie that was finally made was quite different. The schedule was too short and every time they were in danger of going over by 10%, they tore dialogue out of the script to compensate. Eventually, all that was left were shallow characters, blood, and gore. We felt so badly about it that Gloria and I asked to have our names removed from the writing credits. The production company did not comply. Fortunately for them, box office reception was positive both in the United Kingdom and overseas.

■ **1981 — *The History of the World: Part I* — Brooksfilms**

A short interlude of frivolity with Dom DeLuise, Madeline Kahn, Gregory Hines, Pamela Stephenson, Orson Welles, and Spike

Milligan. I did nothing important on this project, just laughed at Mel Brooks' jokes and helped the extras start the French Revolution.

### ■ 1982 – *Britannia Hospital* – EMI

This Lindsay Anderson black comedy was a follow-up from *If* and other satirical movies he directed. It featured Malcolm McDowell, Mark Hamill, Leonard Rossiter, and Robbie Coltrane. I was called in by the special effects supervisor for a sequence where Malcolm McDowell's head is attached to a body made of multiple body parts—a modern Frankenstein of sorts—who then bites the surgeon. In the struggle, the surgeon pulls the head off again. The body proceeds to strangle a nurse before being laid to rest. They asked me to make the prosthetics, the animatronic headless body, the head, a dummy to pump seven gallons of blood, and 160 body parts in three weeks. It seemed totally impossible (as ludicrous as the sequence itself), but I did it anyway, working crazy hours and going home only occasionally. My reputation for doing impossible jobs was growing.

I visited Stuart (Freeborn) at Elstree studios, where he was preparing to do ***Star Wars VI: Return of the Jedi***. It became clear that he was somewhat upset with me for building three versions of Yoda on ***Episode V*** when he had said that could not be done.

The Ewoks had already been designed, and small prototypes had been produced by a toy manufacturer. There was no creativity in copying nylon fur fabric and they were not practical creatures designed for running through a forest. It was very quickly clear that Stu wasn't going to give me the kind of tasks that I was hoping for. And so, sadly, I came to the realization that it was time for me to stand on my own two feet and move away from the classic trilogy.

### ■ 1982 — *Whoops Apocalypse* — London Weekend TV

A British comedy about the last week before doomsday with John Cleese, Richard Griffiths, and Barry Morse where I made the prosthetics used throughout the show.

### ■ 1982 — *The Hunchback of Notre Dame* — Columbia Pictures Corporation/Rosemont Productions

I'm not sure if Norman Rosemont remembered me from previous productions. Probably not. But I was asked to head the makeup department because of my growing reputation as a specialist in prosthetics. That is what they needed for the title character, played by Sir Anthony Hopkins. The movie also starred Derek Jacobi, David Suchet, Sir John Gielgud, Lesley-Anne Down, and Robert Powell. I had the advantage of a very capable primary assistant, Beryl Lerman, who took my direction and then organized all the regular makeup needs so well that I did not need to worry about them. Tony Hopkins was a dream to work with, and I think of this movie with much affection. He was a perfect subject, incredibly cooperative, did his best to take care of the makeup through very long days, and even credited me as "doing all the work" when he was interviewed by ITV News. It was only a five-week shoot with three weeks' preparation time, which is a very short period

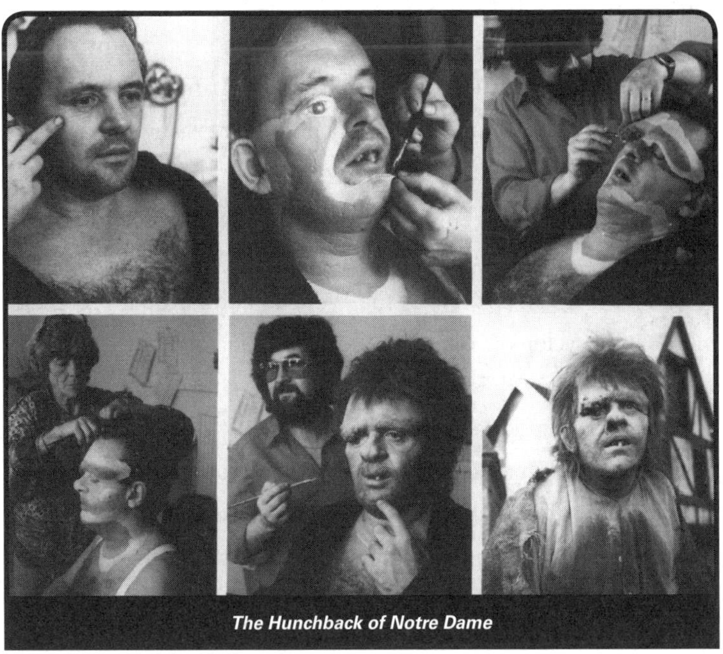

***The Hunchback of Notre Dame***

to prepare enough prosthetic pieces for thirty-plus days of filming. Quasimodo was needed virtually every day, and that meant a new set of prosthetics were required every day. It was a challenging job for which I was rewarded with an Emmy nomination.

### ■ 1983 — *Krull* — Paramount British Pictures

This was the happiest movie I made. Firstly, because the producers were so appreciative and easy to work with. Secondly, because it was the first BIG budget movie that I was designing creature FX for. Thirdly, because they let me do (pretty much) anything I wanted.

I assembled a young crew that could more easily accept me as boss. But there was some conflict with the regular makeup artists, who saw me as something of an upstart. The movie had creature effects of all kinds: prosthetics on the changelings and on Francesca Annis as the Widow of the Web, an animatronic/prosthetic mix for the cyclops (I operated the radio-controlled eye and brow while actor Bernard Bresslaw delivered the dialogue). I designed lenses into the cyclops mask so he could see where he was going. I designed a groundbreaking animatronic creature suit for the Beast and for forty horse-riding Slayers to storm the castle. The movie featured Liam Neeson and Robbie Coltrane in small parts before they became household names. This was the first movie that honored me with a credit in the opening titles.

Nick operating the eye of Real the Cyclops on *Krull*

### ■ 1983 — *Journey to Krull* — Columbia Pictures/Kaleidoscope/ Columbia TriStar Home Entertainment

This was a documentary where they interviewed me about making the Slayers, which were my least favorite creatures in that movie.

### ■ 1983 — *The Keep* — Paramount Pictures

It seems extraordinary that one of my worst movie experiences should follow on the heels of the best. I was still working on the post-production of ***Krull*** in Pinewood Studios when I was offered ***The Keep***, which was setting up in Shepperton Studios fifteen miles away. For a month, I worked days on ***Krull*** and evenings on ***The Keep***. The movie starred Scott Glenn, Jürgen Prochnow, and Gabriel Byrne. My wife, who did the preliminary read-through of the script, marking sequences I needed to take particular note of, advised me not to do the movie. I should have listened to her. Actor Ian McKellen was very professional as I did a makeup simulating a diseased, premature-aging condition on him. But as I tried to focus on the various metamorphosis of the transforming villain, Molisar, writer/director/producer Michael Mann wouldn't listen to technical advice and insisted on pursuing avenues unlikely to produce practical results. I guess the problem was that Michael had a vision that none of us were ever going to realize to his satisfaction, and he kept pursuing it. He changed his mind to such an extent that, once filming started, he was rewriting the script every night for the next day's filming. Chaos reigned and there were eight nervous breakdowns. It was the first time that I questioned whether the politics and stresses of being head of a department outweighed the thrill of seeing your work on screen. The charred, fossilized soldiers in the courtyard worked very well; as did the second version of Molisar's evolution, a spectacular muscle suit. But ultimately, Michael wasn't happy with me and I was equally unhappy with him. After going over schedule by an unheard-of nine months, it was slow and ponderous. The distributors withdrew it from cinemas after only six days for re-editing. Today, it is a hard film to find.

■ **1983 – *Screamtime* aka *Dreamhouse* – Salon Productions**

I slit someone's throat (and a few other makeup effects).

■ **1983 – *Grizzly II: The Concert* – Predator Ltd**

These were Charlie Sheen and George Clooney's first speaking movie roles, I believe. Laura Dern was a young performer who joined veterans Louise Fletcher and John Rhys-Davies; but despite that, this is perhaps the worst movie I contributed to. It was fraught with financial problems from the start. Building an eight-foot animatronic bear and a sixteen-foot marionette while trying to keep the crew paid brought many anxious moments. We filmed in communist Hungary. The Hungarian crew wouldn't let us use their workshop and insisted that they build whatever we needed. That culminated in a blood pump exploding under pressure, which covered John Rhys-Davies, the director, continuity girl, and sound and camera crews with sticky fake blood. I was not popular that day. We completed and tested the half-sized, false-perspective animatronic bear just before the movie folded. So we never got to shoot those sequences. The Hungarian authorities seized our personal equipment against the company's unpaid bills and we never got any of it back. Years later, I saw the film had somehow been completed. I watched the first reel. It was worse than I imagined.

### 1984 – *Scream for Help* – Torremodo Films Ltd

I was contracted as makeup effects consultant, making FX heads for this movie. It was a particularly unusual situation as my wife, Gloria, had previously been a girlfriend of the cigar-puffing director, Michael Winner, of ***Death Wish*** fame.

### 1984 – *Wild Boys* (Music Video) – EMI

I was called in by the makeup supervisor to do prosthetic and animatronic effects on this extraordinary video featuring the rock band Duran Duran. We had only ten days to prepare, so di-

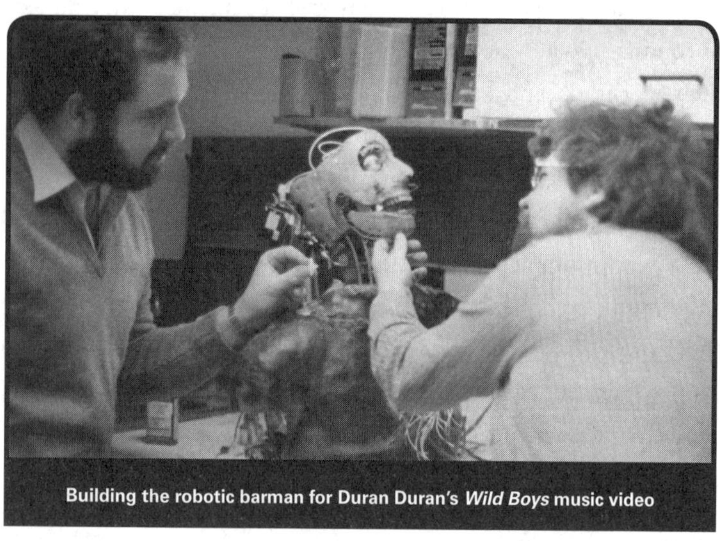

Building the robotic barman for Duran Duran's *Wild Boys* music video

rector Russell Mulcahy gave me a free hand to make whatever I could in that time and adapt things I already had. This was a breath of fresh air. My crew and I did prosthetics, bald heads, and airbrushed facial and body makeups on about thirty dancers. We created the fire-breathing robotic barman, too. The shoot was very fluid and innovative, and Russell and I developed a great working relationship. It was suggested that the band thought there were too many special effects and not enough focus on the band. Maybe that changed when we won the Grammy for Best Video that year.

### ■ 1985 – *Lifeforce* – London Cannon Films

Without a doubt, this movie has the biggest array of complex creature effects of any movie that I made. Unfortunately, it was a story of soul-sucking vampires from outer space that nobody could take seriously at the time. It starred Steve Railsback, Peter Firth, Frank Finlay, the then virtually unknown Patrick Stewart (***Star Trek***'s Captain Picard) and the adorable, usually naked Mathilda May. Director Tobe Hooper was very easy to work with. He allowed me to work directly with writer Dan O'Bannon to rework transformation and effects sequences throughout the movie, which allowed me to maximize effect and minimize budget. Then he let me direct my own "animatronics unit" to film those sequences that I had devised. I had a huge crew of almost seventy assistants, and my work is apparent every five to ten minutes through this film. For the destruction of London, I used seven novice crew members to put 175 zombies on the streets over five nights. ***Thriller*** had used thirty artists to produce thirty zombies. Those novices all went on to have distinguished careers. The Pathologist transformation sequence is worthy of particular note, as I filmed that in real time with two animatronic dummies morphing in the same shot. This was long before the use of computer graphics. Tobe kept telling me, "You'll get an Oscar for this, Nick," and once again I was given credit in the opening titles. But unfortunately, the critics couldn't handle the combination of sex and zombies. They slated the movie, but our FX won a Saturn award.

**Nick adding final details of the vampire bat creature moments before Jim Henson's surprise visit**

**■ 1985 — Arena: An Absurd Notion (Video Album) — EMI**

A video album with Duran Duran based around, and including, the *Wild Boys* video.

**■ 1985 — *Seitenstechen* — Lisa Films GmBh Munich**

A quick trip to Germany to make comedian Mike Krüger pregnant.

**■ 1985 — *The Making of* Lifeforce — London Canon Films**

This documentary focused on the work of myself and optical effects designer John Dykstra. It contains thirty minutes of details on how we created miniature sets, optical illusions, vampires, zombies, explosions, and transformations.

**■ 1986 — *Highlander* — 20th Century Fox/EMI Films/Highlander Productions Limited**

I think this was the best movie that I designed creature FX for—but it was a nightmare to make. It starred Christopher Lambert, Sean Connery, and Clancy Brown, and continued my working relationship with Director Russell Mulcahy. Russell was a delight to work with, and we fed off each other's ideas. When I pointed out that the five beheadings were very repetitive, he gave me latitude to design the storyboards for all the Quickening sequences. I built the tension in each sequence by revealing more each time another head rolled. I completed all the beheadings and designed and fabricated the prosthetics. But the producers made a number of choices that impacted my department badly. When they recast the Scottish heroine, they failed to give me the thirteen weeks of preparation time for Heather's aging prosthetics, which led to a two-dimensional makeup that I strongly opposed. They moved the movie to derelict dockland near Tower Bridge in the heart of London, which added two hours travel time to my day. They failed to get Clancy Brown to shave his head as I requested, which added another two hours of prosthetics to my day. As a result, I found myself stressed and exhausted, working 110-hour weeks (sixteen hours a day, seven days a week). The hassles of budget, schedules, and politics combined with extreme fatigue pushed me to the edge. The final straw came when cinematographer Gerry Fisher refused to accept that I (someone with a makeup union card) would direct second unit. He created an impossible and unworkable atmosphere. I have often wondered what I could have done to avoid that situation. Perhaps I should have been less ambitious, or maybe I should have been less caring. If I had held back and given less of myself to the job, would that have avoided the situation? Either way, exhaustion, both physical and emotional, overwhelmed me and I was unable to continue.

■ **1988 – I directed *Tourism Awareness* – ABS TV Antigua**

A public information film.

■ **1990 – I directed *Visage* – ABS TV**

A fashion short.

■ **1992**

I was stage designer for a preliminary round of the **Miss World Pageant** in Antigua and Barbuda, and was honored to be one of the judges for that competition.

■ **1993**

I was stage designer for **Calvin S' Anniversary Show**: a fashion extravaganza at the Chinese Cultural Center in Antigua.

■ **1994**

I was stage designer for **Darkside of the Catwalk** fashion show for Black n' Black Productions. It involved catwalks on multi-levels.

■ **1994**

I also directed the video presentation of **Darkside of the Catwalk** - Black n' Black Productions, Antigua.

Yoda Guy Movie Exhibit

## ■ 1994

I directed ***Calvin S***, an Island Arts/Black n' Black Production. This was a TV presentation with beautiful fashions contrasted against the huge machinery of a derelict sugar factory.

## ■ 1995

I returned to Los Angeles to direct two music videos for Living Values Corporation, LA USA/Alien Artists.

**When You Call** - Featuring singer/songwriter Toma.

**Best of Both Worlds** - Prosthetic effects turned Toma into sixteen different characters. The video was a Worldfest Huston Film Festival winner in 1996.

## ■ 1996

I designed the stage for **Antigua Carnival '96** - Government of Antigua.

## ■ 2011

I became the Curator of the **Yoda Guy Movie Exhibit** in Sint Maarten, listed on TripAdvisor as the most popular "thing to do" in Philipsburg, the capital city.

■ **2016 — *Under ConTROLL* aka *Goblin 2* — German Production Company: Merkurfilm Baden-Baden**

A very short stint as creature effects consultant to creature designer Jörg Steegmüller explaining the basics of movie animatronics.

■ **2017 — *The Galaxy Britain Built* — BBC World**

I met with the BBC at Celebration Europe in 2016, and they followed me to Sint Maarten to complete my section of this excellent documentary. It was an interesting look at how ***Star Wars*** started as an under-budget project and the versatility of the British artists who fleshed out that world. I talked about the making of the creatures for the Mos Eisley cantina sequence in ***Star Wars IV***, and they filmed me working on rebuilding a Yoda puppet.

■ **2018 — *A World War II Fairytale: The Making of Michael Mann's* The Keep**

As if living through ***The Keep*** wasn't bad enough the first time, the makers of this documentary were obsessed with telling the story of our challenging experience. They caught up with me while I was working in Germany and interviewed me about that movie's dark challenges.

STAR WARS
NICK MALEY
Official Pix
STAR WARS
CELEBRATION

## POSTSCRIPT

Gee but it's great to be famous,
to enter a room to applause,
to see their respect and attention,
and receive admiration ...

like yours.

But one thing that fills me with panic,
as nervous as nervous can be ...
What in the world's gonna happen,
if they ever find out ...
I'm just me!

# BOOK GUIDE

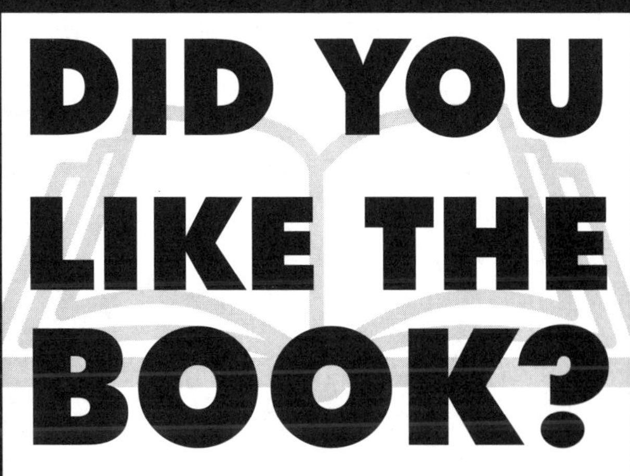


Rate it and share your opinion.

amazon.com

BARNES&NOBLE
BOOKSELLERS
www.bn.com

## *Not what you expected? Tell us!*

**Most negative reviews occur when the book did not reach expectation. Did the description build any expectations that were not met? Let us know how we can do better.**

**Please drop us a line at *info@fhautism.com*.**
**Thank you so much for your support!**